GV 950.5 .B35 2007
B. . . . . . e.
T. . . . . terback
playbook

P9-DDW-486

WITHDRAWN
UNIVERSITY LIBRARY
THE UNIVERSITY OF TEXAS RIO GRANDE VALLEY

LIBRARY
THE UNIVERSITY OF TEXAS
AT BROWNSVILLE
Brownsville, Tx 78520-4991

THE ARMCHAIR QUARTERBACK PLAYBOOK

THE ARMCHAIR QUARTERBACK PLAYBOOK

The Ultimate Guide to Watching Football

CHRISTOPHER LEE BARISH

LIBRARY
THE UNIVERSITY OF TEXAS
AT BROWNSVILLE
Brownsville, Tx 78520-4991

CHRONICLE BOOKS
SAN FRANCISCO

Text copyright © 2007 by Christopher Lee Barish. Illustrations copyright © 2007 by Mike Essl.
All rights reserved. No part of this book may be reproduced in any form without written permission
from the publisher.

Library of Congress Cataloging-in-Publication Data available.

ISBN-10: 0-8118-5928-2
ISBN-13: 978-0-8118-5928-8

Manufactured in Canada

Designed by Mike Essl
Design Assistance by Louise Ma and Richard Watts

Distributed in Canada by Raincoast Books
9050 Shaughnessy Street
Vancouver, British Columbia V6P 6E5

10 9 8 7 6 5 4 3 2 1

Chronicle Books LLC
680 Second Street
San Francisco, California 94107

www.chroniclebooks.com

INTRODUCTION

"Armchair Quarterback." The phrase speaks of poise in the recliner, pinpoint remote control, and the will to watch hours and hours of football in the face of an obtrusive roommate, a needy child, or an unrelenting mother-in-law. It's all about having the intestinal fortitude to devour 24 nuclear wings, with or without blue cheese, in a single quarter. It's all about the willingness to undergo epic struggles to escape prior commitments when the game seems all but lost, and the heart-pumping adrenaline to lead teammates from channel to channel and game to game with picture-in-picture. It's all about an icy winter Monday night, standing on the frozen deck, puffing on a halftime cigar, lips purple from the bitter cold, and it's all about the ability to reach deep inside—and stay inside—to continue watching a fourth-quarter blowout on a glorious fall afternoon despite a shower of criticism. To family and friends, he's as fine a gentleman as they'd ever want to meet, but in the armchair, he'll rip an opponent's heart out.

Imagine a world without Armchair Quarterbacks. On football-season Saturdays and Sundays, instead of working on their game, they would be inhabiting far too many county fairs with their significant others, causing undue strain in their relationships. Mondays at work, what would the topic of conversation be? Would men riff on the intricacies of English cricket? And being fluent in football is a valuable social skill. One can talk game at job interviews it offers patter with the relatives, and it's suitable conversation with the other guy on a double date.

The AQ was born on October 22, 1939, when NBC aired the nation's first televised professional football game a Philadelphia Eagles defeat of the Brooklyn Dodgers 23-14. A few fortunate New Yorkers—a mere 500 who owned TV sets and loved football—were able to witness the game from the comfort of their own recliners. They had the game-watching vision that set the framework for AQs today.

The advent of AQing presented unquestioned benefits The AQ didn't need to drive to the game and fight traffic, or chase a train; he could simply walk a few steps to the living room. He no longer had to purchase tickets to watch the game; he just had to switch his TV on. He didn't have to buy stadium concessions; he could survive on foodstuffs from his own kitchen. Rather than sit on hard metal stands or in stadium seating, he could elax in his comfy armchair. He didn't need binoculars o see the action; instead, he was given a spectacular close-up view, which made the game much easier to analyze, scrutinize, and enjoy. And the weather was always just right.

AQ ingenuity couldn't be slowed down. In the early 1950s, Zenith produced the world's first remote control, a breakthrough luxury. This device enabled AQs to turn the game on or change the channel while seated. They could even turn up the game's volume if outside noise, such as that of a spouse or the family, necessitated such action. Next came restaurant delivery. A player could nourish himself with a delicious meal by making a simple phone call, never having to burn his game energy in the kitchen or waste game time by having to leave the field of play in search of food. Then, cable TV brought thousands more hours of game time. By 1985, we began to see a clear composite of the modern AQ. Today, whatever breakthroughs await us, one thing is certain: the position will continue to evolve.

This resource contains offensive plays and defensive schemes to help maximize your game and ensure you're fully equipped to combat any obstacle. It also includes advice on equipment, delicious game food recipes, how-to lists, TD dances, accepted AQ etiquette, relevant football watching information, a thorough Resource Section and AQ vernacular (a glossary of lingo to expand on the italicized terms found throughout this book).

Attack, argue, and strategize. Beg and bitch. Intimidate. Invest. A gifted AQ does whatever it takes in his relentless march toward destiny. And, equipped with *The Armchair Quarterback Playbook*, he is destined to succeed.

THE CHRONOLOGY OF ARMCHAIR QUARTERBACKING

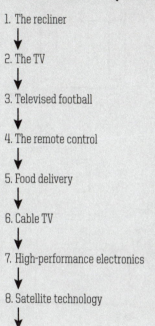

1. The recliner

2. The TV

3. Televised football

4. The remote control

5. Food delivery

6. Cable TV

7. High-performance electronics

8. Satellite technology

9. DVR

PLAY DIAGRAM SYMBOLS

ARMCHAIR QUARTERBACK

RECLINER

TV

REMOTE CONTROL

BEER

COFFEE TABLE

SIGNIFICANT OTHER / OPPONENT

MOTHER-IN-LAW

CHILD

CHILD AQ

PHONE OPERATOR

CAP

HOAGIE

TIMER DIAL

PHONE

BBQ

OTTOMAN

PAPER TOWEL ROLL

CHIP BOWL

WINGS

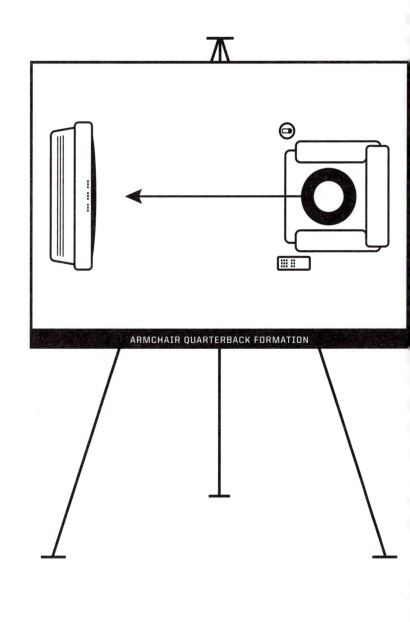

ARMCHAIR QUARTERBACK FORMATION

CHAPTER 1

SOLO PLAYS

To maximize your game, there are mental and physical plays you will need to execute throughout the season. Maybe it's coming down with a painfully effective Down and In to counterattack a Sunday brunch with your parents. Perhaps you're stuck at a flea market and need to run a hurry-up Bitch and Break. To maintain peak performance, you can stay in game shape by strengthening your lateral remote-controlling with simple Clicker Snaps or push your limits with an awe-inspiring Invisible La-Z-Boy.

ESCAPE ROUTES

It seems weddings, birthdays, and funerals always come up at the worst time—game time. Run these escape routes to evade your prior commitments with a clear conscience.

■■

THE DOWN AND IN

PLAY STRATEGY: You're in a tough bind—it's a game day, yet you're penciled in to attend a lesser event. Too bad you've suddenly fallen ill. Make it clear that you'd love to attend the affair, but, unfortunately, you've been shut down by illness, you are perhaps contagious, and the doctor has advised you to stay in.

COACHING POINT
When feigning illness, sniffles and coughs are predictable. Offering up a severe migraine can be more effective and difficult to challenge—plus, they are recurring, which can come in handy for future conflicts.

THE DOWN AND OUT

PLAY STRATEGY: You never know when the doldrums are going to hit—oh here they come! Earnestly explain how you really wish you could make the event, but, sadly, you've been feeling down, and you don't want to subject anybody to your misery—you just need some time for yourself.

COACHING POINT
If you can make the claim that you've been diagnosed with depression, you can have this mentally crippling affliction in your back pocket for life.

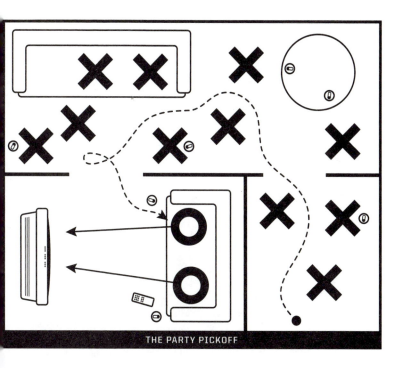

THE PARTY PICKOFF

THE PARTY PICKOFF

PLAY STRATEGY: The game is almost on, and you're stuck at a dreadful party with relatives or at a lame singles bash with your buddies. Follow your instincts and slip away immediately. You might even encounter another wayward AQ wearing the same intense game face. Allow the football magnetism to draw you in until you accidentally stumble on an unoccupied room with a TV.

THE BITCH AND BREAK

PLAY STRATEGY: No one likes to be around a jerk in a bad mood. Create a negative vibe—complain loudly about your life or the world, curse more than usual, talk trash about another person, maybe throw in a few threats of violence. Before you know it, those around you will prefer that you simply go away.

LIBRARY
THE UNIVERSITY OF TEXAS
AT BROWNSVILLE
Brownsville, Tx. 78520

THE HITCH AND BREAK

PLAY STRATEGY: As an AQ, it is within your rights to exit a wedding soon after the vows are exchanged to get home for the game. Go ahead—you've witnessed the important part, and that's what matters most. Sure, weddings are a big deal. But divorces happen all the time, and a big game is played only once. Maybe you'll be able to last all the way through their next wedding.

AQ FUNDAMENTALS
Escape Routes

- Do not schedule weddings, funerals, birthday parties, or business meetings on a big game day. If people don't show up to your wedding because they're watching the game, it's nobody's fault but your own. However, you may plan an event during the championship of another, lesser, sport to show the world how nothing else matters but football.

- If you're pushed into an untimely event by a significant other or your family, you may agree to attend if the game will be on TV and you will be permitted to watch it unfettered.

- If a game day has been planned in advance, under no circumstances should you cancel plans with your teammates—whether for a date, work, or anything else. However, if your date is a *she-Q* who has "made the conversion" (see page 56), you are always welcome to bring her to the gathering.

- If you're stuck somewhere, you may call a friend for updates—or, by all means, check scores on a cell phone, a handheld gadget, or even an old-school transistor radio. Try not to make any noise if you are checking the score during a quiet moment, such as during wedding vows or a eulogy.

AUDIBLE
Burning a Team Logo into Your Lawn

1. Map out the desired size you want the logo on your lawn to be. Outline it so that the letters/images are in proportion to those elements in your team's official logo.

2. Pour Liquid Grass or Root Killer in the pattern of your outlined team logo.

3. Wait until new growth occurs, or until grass turns brown, depending on the substance applied.

4. Paint the logo with colored chalk powder.

5. Stand proud.

THE COFFIN CORNER

PLAY STRATEGY: When a big game is threatened by an untimely event that backs you into a corner, such as a funeral, you must ask yourself, "How well did I really know the guy?" Was he or she a distant family member, a friend of a friend, or just a work acquaintance? After proper consideration, make the tough decision.

COACHING POINT
Funerals are a sad part of life. But celebrating those who have passed away is not. It helps you remember that your time on this planet is limited and that you should enjoy life to the fullest every day. Mourn the deceased, and reaffirm your love of the game on their behalf.

SEPARATION OF CHURCH AND GAME

Whether it lands on Friday, Saturday, or Sunday, the Sabbath can seriously get in the way of a good game. Thank God there are ways around it. Here's how to keep your faith and still make time for religious obligations.

THE HOLY HOOKUP

PLAY STRATEGY: Charity is fundamental in church teachings, and the church loves gifts. That's why you and the fellow AQs of the congregation have decided to pitch in and buy a TV and satellite to be hooked up in your place of worship. Mount it in the meeting room, the community area, or the crying room for all to congregate around during or after services. It's time to pass the plate for something truly sacred—football.

THE AMISH OPTION

PLAY STRATEGY: The Amish live in a society where modern dress and television are often restricted. So how are you supposed to wear team gear and watch a football broadcast under such laws? Easy—during "rumspringa," of course! At 16 years old, many Amish teenagers are permitted the freedom to explore the customs of the "English" world—which includes armchair quarterbacking—before deciding whether or not to join the church for life. Use this time to find yourself and your game. Slip on a team jersey, scarf down an order of chicken wings, place a bet, kick back, and watch a football contest. See if you like it, then make the decision.

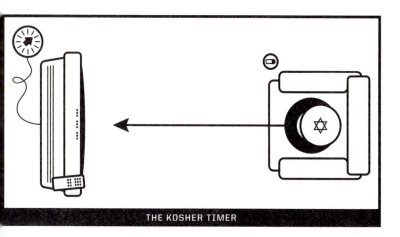

THE KOSHER TIMER

THE KOSHER TIMER

PLAY STRATEGY: Many Jews are forbidden to manipulate electricity on the Sabbath, which can really cut into a man's NCAA football viewing. In this case, prior to the Sabbath, you can set up an electric timer that will switch the game on and off on its own. According to the laws of Judaism, this practice is acceptable, and practice makes perfect.

TRAINING DRILLS

Stay in top game shape by working out the muscles you'll be using during the season. Use these exercises to improve finger flexibility and wrist strength so that you can wield the remote control with deft precision into the playoffs and bowl games.

■■■

THE FINGER FLEX

PLAY STRATEGY: During a typical game, you can make thousands of intricate finger movements. Over the grinding wear and tear of the season, underworked digits could result in finger fatigue, sloppy remote controlling, or, worse, *clicker finger*. Some plagued by this malady are reduced to the point where they must grant control to a visiting AQ a potentially humiliating situation.

Use the following Finger Flex exercises to improve your fingers' flexibility and dexterity:

· Touch your right-hand fingers to your right thumb and your left-hand fingers to your left thumb, one at a time.

· Stretch and flex your clicker fingers.

· Walk the fingers of each hand along a flat surface, like a spider.

· Do three sets of 20 reps of each exercise before each game.

AUDIBLE
Football Anger Management

Watching a game can make you angry. When calls go against your team, you're unhappy with a play, or your team loses, it's natural to get hot-headed. But the stress that comes with it isn't healthy. Here are some AQ anger-management tips:

· Consider this: will the play that makes you angry matter five years from now? Obviously, this depends on the severity of the call and the importance of the game, and how much cash is riding on it.

· Alternatively, consider this: what if it were you who made the wrong call or ran the horrible play? We're all human—even bad referees and incompetent coaches. Forgive them (though you may wish them bad luck in their other endeavors).

· Before you throw the TV out the window or take out your fury on some-body else, count to 10 and take a deep breath between each number. The anger may not be gone, but this can help relax you and reduce the harm you might inflict.

· Close your eyes and visualize a better game result—a thrilling victory next week, a championship season, the maiming of an opposing quarterback.

THE INVISIBLE LA-Z-BOY

PLAY STRATEGY: Build your thighs and calves, tone your buttocks, and reduce stress by creating your own invisible recliner.

1. Stand with your legs squared, about shoulder width apart. Keep your arms straight down.

2. Bend your knees and squat into a chair position.

3. Inhale through your nose, hold the pose as long as you can, let your breath out, and stand up.

4. Marvel at your athleticism.

COACHING POINT
As this drill mostly works the thighs, it will leave your hands free to grip a beer and the remote control as you would in an actual recliner.

AUDIBLE
How to Curse at a Ref in Nine Languages

ENGLISH   You are a shitty referee!

SPANISH   ¡Usted es un árbitro de mierda!

FRENCH   Vous êtes morceau d'arbitre de merde!

DUTCH   U bent stuk van shitscheidsrechter!

GERMAN   Sie sind Stück des Scheißereferenten!

ITALIAN   Siete parte dell'arbitro della merda!

SWEDISH   Du är lappar av skiten domare!

HEBREW   Ata evair! Ata manyak benzona!

JAPANESE   それはひどい支配である!!

CLICKER SNAP

PLAY STRATEGY: The football season is a marathon, not a hundred-yard sprint. During a typical college- and pro-football year you'll remote-control through hundreds of game hours. That's why training and preparation are essential. Improve your wrist strength with the following Clicker Snap.

1. Grip the clicker with your hand.

2. Extend your arm straight out in front of you.

3. Slowly snap your wrist up and down, using the weight of the clicker to flex your wrist muscle.

4. Do three sets of 20 reps before or during each game.

5. Kick some ass.

THE PRAYER POSE

PLAY STRATEGY: How well do you handle the pressures of a tight game? Are you cool as Montana, or does your inability to cope bring on mental anguish, muscle tension, and a woozy stomach? Whether you are praying for your team or not, this relaxation technique helps you maintain your composure and remain centered in the face of adversity.

1. Sit cross-legged on your chair.

2. Put your palms together in prayer position, with your thumbs touching the center of your chest. Keep your elbows at your sides and your shoulders back.

3. Inhale the aroma of chicken wings and exhale with deep, slow breaths.

4. Relax.

AUDIBLE
How to Calm a Rapid Heartbeat During Overtime

If you feel or hear your heart beating rapidly or are experiencing a fluttering sensation in your chest, follow these steps:

1. Move to a quiet setting.

2. Shut your eyes.

3. Inhale and exhale slowly. Take deep breaths.

4. Focus on relaxing things. Bathe in the splendor of football's competitiveness, athleticism, unpredictability, and legalized violence.

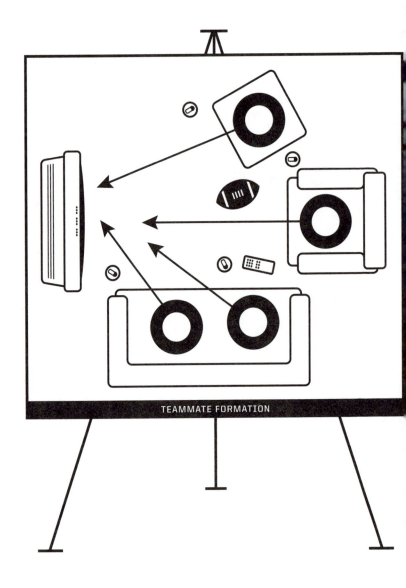

TEAMMATE FORMATION

CHAPTER 2

TEAMMATE PLAYS

Watching the game with teammates has its own set of rules, conduct, and plays. Responsibilities are granted. Jobs are divvied. Results are expected. It's a team effort. But when it's game time, sides are taken, emotions are tweaked, and plays must be made. You might execute a perfectly timed Chest Bump, fire off a Hoagie Throw, or partake in a smooth halftime Game Cigar. Maybe you'll deliver a crushing insult or use a patronizing Sympathy Voice regarding your buddy's team, bust into an Ickey Shuffle, or even get called for a penalty, such as an Accidental Jinxing or a Premature Mock. And, by the way, where the hell is the Beer Bitch? (See chapter 5, Game Food.)

Use whatever it takes to be a leader, a respected team-mate, and a game-day force.

VISITING PLAYS

Be a classy visiting teammate and show your gratitude by bearing game offerings for the home AQ. Just remember—nobody likes a *cheap shot*.

■■■

THE GAME CIGAR

PLAY STRATEGY: If you want to be a welcome guest, graciously bring along a couple high-quality cigars to smoke on the porch while you schmooze during time-outs and halftime—fine smaller cigars that can be smoked within the span of a halftime break. For a detailed cigar guide, see the Resource Section, but here's a brief selection of football-friendly stogies.

- *Cigarillo:* A small, thin cigar about ½ inch longer than a cigarette. Cigarillos are sold in quantities of 10 or 20 and are a great cigar choice for a group of buddies on the deck. Smoke time: 5–10 minutes.

- *Panatela:* A thin cigar, approximately 6 inches long, with a ½-inch circumference. Smoke time: 15 minutes.

- *Robusto:* Thick and pudgy, this cigar is approximately 4 inches long and has a circumference of ½ inch. Smoke time: 20–25 minutes.

THE BEER BEHIND

PLAY STRATEGY: Instead of bringing a six-pack of so-so beer along for the group, arrive with a case of high-quality brew, so that, after you leave, a few are left over for the host as a remnant of your generosity.

THE TRIPLE WING

PLAY STRATEGY: Be the ultimate wing connoisseur; show off your eclectic tastes and make an extraordinary effort by bringing as your offering three orders of hot wings—one each of mild, medium, and hot, so that the wings are certain to be devoured by all.

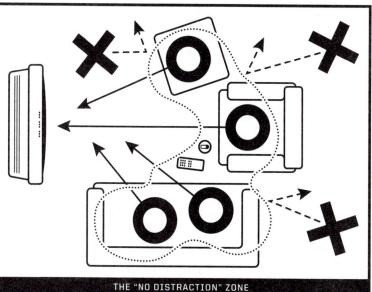

THE "NO DISTRACTION" ZONE

AQ FUNDAMENTALS
Hosting

- You must provide a "No-Distraction Zone" around the game so that you and your teammates can enjoy the broadcasts in peace. This means no barking dogs or obtrusive significant others, children, or roommates. Inside the no-distraction zone, teammates can be as loud or boisterous as they please, with no reprisals.

- Whether you purchase beverages and/or food or they're brought by teammates, as the host, you are ultimately in charge of having enough to last through overtime. (See chapter 5, Game Food, for detailed food and beverage plays.)

- Your game-watching equipment must be in working order. At the very least, your TV must be clearly viewable and the sound clearly audible. (See chapter 6, The Equipment Room.)

SPORTS-BAR PLAYS

By choice or by necessity, you may leave your field of play to watch games at a sports bar—a venue where the local AQs congregate and recreate. There, camaraderie is shared, bravado is on full display, and like in a prison yard, fights between rival factions may break out at any moment. Establish your field position with a tactical Squatter and make your presence felt early. (For America's best sports bars, see the Resource Section.)

■■■

OVERPOWERING YOUR OPPONENTS

PLAY STRATEGY: He who taunts last, taunts hardest. Often, you find yourself pitted against fans rooting for the other team. (You can usually spot them immediately by their game jerseys or by their all-around poor taste.) You must fight your instincts and allow your opponents to mock you first. Then, when your victory is safe in hand, you may deride them mercilessly—after all, they started it. On the other hand, if your team is certain to lose, you may first attack the opposition by calling them "bandwagon fans."

THE BARTENDER'S BUDDY

PLAY STRATEGY: Get to know the bartender early, because he or she is often the one in control of your games. Let him or her know you understand how busy (s)he's going to be. This should give you greater control of the game if a channel change or volume adjustment is necessary. (An AQ with brass footballs might try to sneak in his own universal remote and attempt to operate the games for himself—a high-risk, high-reward play.)

THE INSIDE-OUT TUCK

PLAY STRATEGY: If you feel unhappy with your team's performance or wronged by their front-office moves, wear your team jersey inside out as a public protest. Bad trades, letting players leave to free agency, and raised ticket prices are all valid precursors to the move.

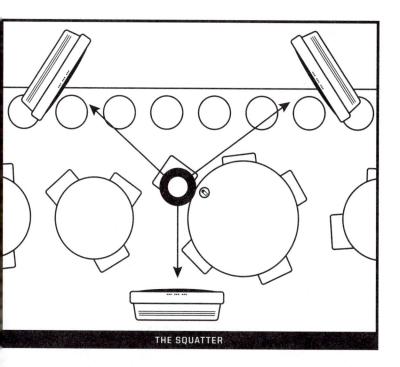

THE SQUATTER

THE SQUATTER

PLAY STRATEGY: For big game days, you—or someone in your party—should arrive at least one hour prior to the first game's kickoff to survey the field and commandeer a prime table. The Squatter should receive proper compensation from his teammates in the form of a free round and appetizer.

THE SPORTING GENTLEMAN

PLAY STRATEGY: When a waitress is serving you, always be gentlemanly, leaving the boorish behavior to the unrefined patrons around you. Sports bars are rife with louts, which will make your distinguished behavior stand out all the more. Treating the waitress right will help ensure that your table's nourishment and gaming needs are being met, and may even net a phone number.

THE IDIOT ROUND

PLAY STRATEGY: If a teammate bursts into a cheer for the wrong team, prematurely mocks another table (see "AQ Penalties," page 35), or fails miserably in an erratic game of Pop-A-Shot in front of other patrons (or, worse, in front of the ladies) he probably has embarrassed you. In such instances, he must take a seat, apologize, and buy a round of drinks.

AQ FUNDAMENTALS
Jerseys

- The player's name on the back of your jersey should be on your team's current roster. The only exceptions are if the player is a past great or if it's a throwback jersey. Also, please make an effort not to wear a team uniform with your own name on the back of the jersey. That's false advertising.

- A jersey should fit its wearer properly. A thin dude swallowed up by a linebacker's shirt or a fat guy squeezed into a running back's just looks wrong.

- Football jerseys should not be worn as regular clothes during the week, or their value is diminished. There is one exception, however, which is the work Friday before the big game on Saturday or Sunday, to show off your football allegiance to those who won't have the pleasure of seeing you at game time.

- It's totally acceptable to believe your team gear is bringing your team luck—especially if you've shelled out an inordinate amount of money for a throwback jersey. But if your team loses a few consecutive games while you're sporting your lucky jersey, you are advised to toss it back in the closet.

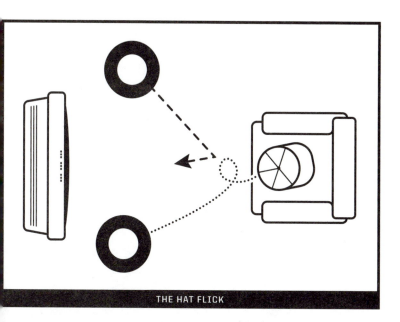

THE HAT FLICK

FIRST-DOWN PLAYS

If you live with roommates or family, you know how critical it is to be first down and in control. Leap out in front with a well-timed Chair Call or run an aggressive Up and Over.

THE HAT FLICK

PLAY STRATEGY: To lay claim to a seat, use your baseball cap like a Frisbee and fling it into the seat of the desired chair from afar. If you're not wearing a hat, you may throw your shoe.

COACHING POINT
Like a passer's aerial attack, this play takes a level of precision and accuracy. During off days, take the time to practice your Hat Flick—it will pay off at game time.

CHAIR CALL

PLAY STRATEGY: "I've got the chair!" Chair Calling can also be leveraged to *retain* the seat. Calling "Place back!" immediately, as one gets up from the good chair to use the bathroom or fetch a beer, is a veteran move. To legitimize the call, all teammates should be present at the time of the announcement, and all disputes must be settled by a game of Rock, Paper, Scissors.

COACHING POINT
You can spot a top-flight AQ as one who can keep a seat all day long, even as the games intensify.

THE UP AND OVER

PLAY STRATEGY: If someone else is also charging for the good seat, come from behind the chair and go up and over the back—an athletic and highly respected play.

THE SLEEPER PLAY

PLAY STRATEGY: How bad do you want it? Show off your physical and mental discipline by sleeping in the sought-after sofa or armchair the night before, so that by morning the prime seat is all yours.

COACHING POINT
When pulling off the Sleeper, feel free to get comfy with your own blanket and pillow, thus cementing your territory. You made your bed, now watch the game in it.

PULLING RANK

PLAY STRATEGY: Who literally *owns* the chair? If it's a chair that you bought and you're desperate to reclaim what's rightfully yours, you may use this power play to seize control—it's irrefutable. Some would call it a cheap move, but then again, there's nothing cheap about purchasing a good seat.

AQ PENALTIES

- *Illegal Talking:* Never start a conversation on third and long with less than two minutes in the half. Don't speak during field goal attempts greater than forty yards in a close game. Hold your tongue on a desperate Hail Mary pass. Stay quiet during an important two-point conversion. Pipe down when a ref's announcing a critical call. Be silent on a fourth and inches. And keep it to yourself during other intense football moments an AQ should inherently understand.

- *Accidental Jinxing:* If you unintentionally hex a team, you must apologize and accept that you will quite possibly be blamed as the cause of your team's defeat if one occurs. Some AQs, in an act of defiance, may intentionally jinx their team, as if to say, "Bring it on!" However, statistics show that this tactic works only about 50 percent of the time.

- *Premature Mocking:* Never prematurely ridicule a fellow AQ about his team's defeat before the game's outcome is certain. Regardless of the game's final score, to presume a victory or a defeat is an infraction, and if the game turns the other way, the mockee may mock the mocker about his premature mock forever.

- *Illegal Screen:* Never block the TV screen. You may risk being tagged by a gnawed chicken wing, or, if the infraction occurs at a critical game point, tackled to the ground.

- *Illegal Return:* When a teammate returns from a run without the deliverables he's been assigned to retrieve—whether intentionally or unintentionally—he will let his teammates down in the ensuing *beer blitz*. It is also an infraction when someone returns from a run with the wrong deliverables, such as bringing ultralight beer when premium dark lager was expected.

MAKESHIFT PLAYS

If you're not first down or if you're with visiting teammates, you must compete for seats. Strike first with a cagey Ottoman Swipe, or else you may be reduced to effecting a Sprawl.

■■■

THE COOLER SEAT

PLAY STRATEGY: If you are seatless, you may employ a cooler in the vicinity of the game, carry it to the *flanker position*, and use it as a seat.

COACHING POINT
Be forewarned: you might end up having to work the Cooler Seat. It serves adequately as an on-the-fly chair, but you will certainly be asked to retrieve beers for the room—an endless cycle of getting up, reaching into the ice to scoop up a beer, stretching to hand it off, and sitting down again.

THE COFFEE-TABLE FOOT

PLAY STRATEGY: When leaning back and watching the game without proper leg support, an AQ may employ the coffee table to do the job, as long as he doesn't knock over any beer or crush food with his hooves. If beer spillage or food destruction occurs as a result of a Coffee-Table Foot, the offender must supply new food for his teammates immediately—preferably high-quality delivery. Also, if the home AQ's significant other is in the vicinity and sees a person executing a Coffee-Table Foot, it is likely she will interfere.

THE DOG FOOT

PLAY STRATEGY: Every AQ deserves a footrest. That's why, if you're leaning back in a seat without one, you may substitute a standing dog in its place. The success of the Dog Foot lies in keeping the dog still. If the dog is starved for attention, that's a good thing; it could conceivably stay still for a quarter or more. But it has its risks—most notably a hyper-extended knee if the dog hears the pizza guy and sprints for the door.

THE OTTOMAN SWIPE

THE OTTOMAN SWIPE

PLAY STRATEGY: If you are stuck without a seat at a large game gathering, swipe the ottoman of another teammate, move it to the *flanker position*, and sit on it. The ottoman swiper must, however, move with his ottoman so that he is not sitting in front of the swipee.

COACHING POINTS
If the swipee is rooting for the opposing team, hastily pulling the ottoman out from under his legs is an opening salvo that can set the stage for a day full of physical and verbal battles between you. Also, because it offers no back support, you may want to position your ottoman against a wall.

THE SPRAWL

PLAY STRATEGY: To acquire seating, an AQ may need to take desperate measures. If all seats are occupied, you can lie down with your back on the floor, facing the game, and use the side of an ottoman or the corner of a couch as a headrest.

COACHING POINT
Never use the Sprawl directly below a lounging teammate. Having your head resting on the floor or against the base of his furniture during a game day can induce severe injury. When a running back breaks one, a teammate could jump to his feet and stomp your gut or even squash your dome.

BASIC TEAMMATE PLAYS

Whether you're blocking or mocking, being a teammate means having everyone's back. Be a playmaker, and be the man.

BLOCKING FOR A TEAMMATE

PLAY STRATEGY: Help your teammate escape his home-field blitz, and welcome him to your field of play. It's good sportsmanship, and the more protection you can offer a fellow AQ, the more you'll get in return. Call the player's spouse and make the play on her sensitive side.

- "He said he'd help me fix my car's fuel injection." (Note: Refer to something technical that she won't understand.) "If I don't get to it today, I can't make it to work on Monday."

- "Me and [significant other] broke up. I really need somebody to talk to, or I might lose it."

- "My dog is really sick. I need some help holding him down so I can give him his medication."

- "I just got laid off, and I'm feeling suicidal."

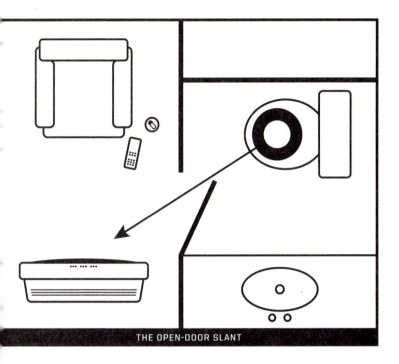

THE OPEN-DOOR SLANT

THE OPEN-DOOR SLANT

PLAY STRATEGY: Leaving your seat in mid-play is never encouraged and is even frowned on. However, when you absolutely must use the bathroom during play, it is acceptable to keep the bathroom door slightly ajar so that you can view the action from the less-esteemed porcelain chair. As teammates, you all have a fundamental right to get a view of the game, no matter where you are. Period.

COACHING POINT
Note that the circumstances are different if you are taking a one instead of a two. Use your eye-hand coordination to keep your eyes fixed on the game—and your hands fixed somewhere else—without committing a messy *bladder lateral.* Another option is to run a "mirrored' Open-Door Slant, wherein the AQ angles the TV so that the game is viewable in the bathroom mirror.

AUDIBLE
Acceptable Talking Points During Blowouts

- Recent crimes committed by players.
- Sexy female sideline reporters.
- Current events, but only if they relate to sports, violence, or sex.
- The fine choreography and *good cheer* from the cheerleaders.
- If you have family, you may want to mention them now.

THE STUD HUG

PLAY STRATEGY: A Stud Hug is acceptable as long as the embrace lasts a brief moment and the affection is kept to no more than one hand on the other's back—accentuated by hard patting. The end of the hug should conclude with a cool handshake or a fist or chest bump (see page 45).

THE SYMPATHY VOICE

PLAY STRATEGY: Use the Sympathy Voice to talk smack to a teammate who's just endured a brutal call or whose team is getting crushed. When your buddy's team catches a tough break, you can certainly understand his pain—that's why it's so important to be as condescending as possible when comforting him. Look deep into the eyes of the loser and patronizingly say, "I feel for you, dude."

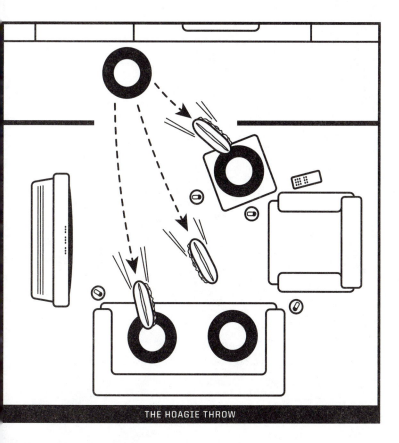

THE HOAGIE THROW

THE HOAGIE THROW

PLAY STRATEGY: When you or a teammate return from a halftime food run with hero sandwiches, deliver incoming grinders with chest-high passes to your seated teammate receivers.

COACHING POINTS:
When attempting to execute this expert aerial maneuver, make certain to snap off a tight spiral. A wobbly or errant throw could trash a room's decor and waste game food, leaving teammates malnourished and edgy. Also, be sure to deliver the Hoagie Throw high above the potential vertical leap of a dog that might be plotting to intercept it.

41

AUDIBLE
How to Throw an Armchair Spiral

At halftime, you may want to step out onto the lawn and toss the pigskin around, or, if you cannot wait, you might be inclined to zip the ball around from your seated positions while watching the game. Here's how to throw the perfect Armchair Spiral:

1. Make sure your fingertips are clean of salsa, onion dip, and beer-bottle condensation, to avoid ball slippage.

2. Loosen your fingers by gently tossing the ball from hand to hand.

3. With the ball's laces facing up, place your ring finger and pinkie along the seams. Place your index finger on the tip of the ball, and curve your thumb and middle fingers under and around the ball. Don't grip it too tightly.

4. Hold the football high, with your elbow level with your shoulder.

5. Visualize a tackle coming at you at full speed.

6. Lean back in your armchair to avoid an imaginary tackle, then release the pass with a forward motion toward the intended teammate. To avoid a wobbly throw, let the ball roll off your fingertips.

7. Hear the spiral whiz past your ear.

8. If you throw three consecutive ducks, you may claim to have a jammed finger from fixing a shelf or an engine part.

THE *MINTERCEPTION*

PLAY STRATEGY: Beer, blue cheese, cigars—when an AQ is down in the trenches all day, his breath can get brutally rank, a rare strain of halitosis called "Armchair Quarterback breath." Try to have mints or gum on you so that nobody gets gassed in the huddle. Throat lozenges are a good idea as well: after you spend a full day of hollering plays, they can help keep your voice strong when you're barking cadence.

PHONE PLAYS

During game time, making or receiving phone calls is generally forbid-den—unless you're engaging your teammates or harassing them, which are both encouraged. Of course, in a perfect AQ world, teammates would be together so that there is no need for a Phone Play. Here are legal and effective ball calls.

■■

THE LIVE FEED

PLAY STRATEGY: Call your pals at home if you are attending the game live—especially at critical points in the game, and when the crowd is at its loudest. The Live Feed is especially important if the game isn't on local TV.

COACHING POINT
If the Live Feeder is lucky enough to be caught by the camera and broadcast on TV, he should not act like a moron, embarrassing himself and the ball callers he represents.

THE BLOWOUT HELLO

PLAY STRATEGY: When your team is winning by more than 31 points at halftime, you may call a friend who is rooting for the other team and annoyingly touch base. Do not gloat, however. Merely by calling him, you are rubbing it in; this is not a time for the Sympathy Voice (see page 40). Just be cool—even clichéd—and say there's still plenty of game left. Some-times your target will concede to you; other times, he may show contempt for you.

AUDIBLE
End Zone Dance Moves

If your team breaks the plane, you can celebrate—and get some exercise, to boot. Here are classic, easy-to-follow touchdown steps to woo the crowd and dazzle the damsels:

The Funky Chicken
(Billy "White Shoes" Johnson, Houston Oilers, 1970s)

1. Raise the ball over your head and wave it around.

2. Pivot your knees in and out like scissors.

The Ickey Shuffle
(Ickey Woods, Cincinnati Bengals, 1980s)

1. Place the football in your left hand.

2. Extend your left arm straight out.

3. Shuffle your left foot twice.

4. Transfer the ball to your right hand.

5. Extend your right arm straight out.

6. Shuffle your right foot twice.

The Mile-High Salute
(Terrell Davis, Denver Broncos, late 1990s)

1. Tuck your arms at your sides.

2. Look straight ahead.

3. Keep your heels together at a 45-degree angle.

4. Turn about-face toward your teammates.

5. Lift your right hand and hold to your slightly arched right eyebrow, as if shading your eyes.

THE CHEST BUMP

The Dirty Bird
(Atlanta Falcons, 1998)

1. Hop up and begin to prance.

2. Fold your arms into a "wing" position.

3. Flap your wings.

The Chest Bump
(unknown origin)

1. Face your teammate and stand approximately 4 feet apart.

2. Both of you arch your chest forward.

3. Simultaneously jump up and against each other's chest.

Note: Chest-bumping a heavier, taller, or uncoordinated teammate can cause injury.

THE ONE RING

PLAY STRATEGY: Call a friend up when you see his favorite team has made a horrific play; let it ring once, then hang up. This will let him know you're watching. As his team spirals downward, the more One Rings you can mount on a person, the more piercing it is.

COACHING POINT
To ensure that the One Ring is not used against you, turn your phone off immediately after your team makes a costly play.

AUDIBLE
The East Coast-West Coast Feud

West Coast advantages:

- Morning start times get you into the games early.
- Earlier end times enable more healing time for work or school.
- Bloody Marys.
- Game food.
- Beer.

East Coast advantages:

- Later start time allows time for sleeping late, running errands, and taking part in religious observations.
- Later start time offers games into night.
- Bloody Marys.
- Game food.
- Beer.

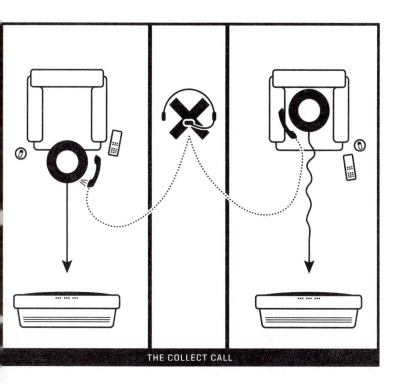

THE COLLECT CALL

THE COLLECT CALL

PLAY STRATEGY: Place a collect call to a friend, posing as a football player who has just made a devastating play against your friend's team. Bringing a third party (the operator) into the mix takes longer to execute than a One Ring, but that's what makes it sting even more.

COACHING POINT
If the operator knows you're not a professional football player—because he, too, is watching the game and refuses to help you with the play—politely hang up and call another operator.

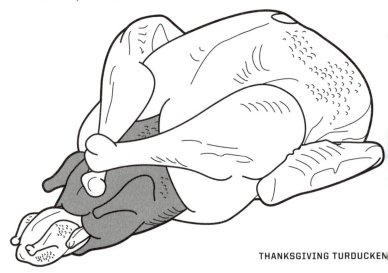

THANKSGIVING TURDUCKEN

HOLIDAY PLAYS

Every year, AQs nationwide are thankful for Thanksgiving football. It's stupefying that the Pilgrims and the Native Americans had the foresight to create a holiday just for watching the game. On this splendid day, if you are fortunate, your game experience comes catered with home cooked meals laboriously prepared by significant others who feel obliged to serve you and clean up after you.

■■■

THANKSGIVING FOOTBALL TRADITIONS

- Though your feast may be at a dinner-table setting, the game must always be audible from a TV in another room.

- It is proper to have second-string TVs in the kitchen or the dining area for constant viewage.

- As soon as one guy takes his Thanksgiving foodstuffs into the TV room to watch the game, it is okay for every guy to start *flooding the field*.

- When watching the game together, you no longer have to speak with family members, or, if you do, you are permitted to speak only of football.

- After meals, the *unbutton hook* and subsequent couch slouching, often considered slovenly by your opponents during regular-season games, is traditional on this day.

GOING BOWLING

The holiday season is a time for sharing, being with your loved ones, and watching 30 college bowl games. There's cheeriness in the December air, the stockings are on the mantelpiece, and championship games are on nearly every day of the week through the entire month (except for NFL Sundays, of course). And if you can take in the entire back-to-back-to-back-to-back New Year's Day bowl marathon, you'll begin your year with a superlative AQ rating.

AUDIBLE
What's Your AQ Rating?

A veteran AQ watches hundreds of football telecasts every season. Consider the multitiered slate of games on *NFL Sunday, Monday Night Football,* NCAA Fridays, Saturdays and college bowl games, local high school championships, arena leagues, Canadian football, NFL Europe, and NFL Network, which features football programming 24/7/365. Use the following chart to calculate your approximate experience level:

AQ Career	Experience (hours)	Rating
5 years	360-1,800	Phenom
10 years	720-3,600	Veteran
20 years	1,440-7,200	All-Pro
30 years	2,160-14,400	Legend

SUPER BOWL MONDAY

PLAY STRATEGY: When NFL playoffs begin, about six weeks prior to the Super Bowl, put in for a personal leave at work for the Monday after the game. Everyone says the Super Bowl is now a holiday, so treat it like one. Enjoy the gorging and the partying without having to go through the Super Bowl Sunday Night Funk. And because you'll probably be the only one with the day off, feel free to throw a few digs at your teammates' lack of foresight.

ARMCHAIR QUARTERBACK LEGENDS
James Henry Smith (1950-2005)

James Henry Smith took his AQing into eternity. Smith would nourish his teammates every Sunday with freshly prepared chili and hot sausages. He was so devoted that, upon his passing, Smith's family chose to have his friends and relatives pay their last respects to him while his body was posed as if he were doing what he loved most: watching the Pittsburgh Steelers on his high-definition TV, leaning back in his recliner with a beer in one hand and the remote in the other.

Joe Vitelli (October 2003)

Joe Vitelli was an AQ who had his priorities straight. When he learned his girlfriend's sorority formal would keep him from his game, he called a remarkable play. A cunning strategist, Vitelli faked a broken leg for weeks in advance—cast and crutches included—to escape the ill-timed dance. This exceptional play even earned him a grand prize from a TV sports show.

President George W. Bush (January 2002)

From the comfort of his White House AQ zone, President Bush spent a relaxing winter Sunday in the throes of a much-heated NFL playoff game: the Miami Dolphins versus the Baltimore Ravens. The president stood up and cheered, then choked on a pretzel. He fainted and fell face-first into the floor, inflicting an abrasion to his cheek and bruising his lower lip. Even with his injuries, the AQ Bush checked back in to complete the game.

POSTGAME PLAYS

After a draining weekend of AQing, your body badly needs rest. Sit back and relax, catch some highlights, take a quick nap—you certainly deserve it. However, now might be a good time to do your postgame analysis. Review the game (stellar plays, poor coaching strategies, horrible calls, updated standings, and so on) so you are readily prepared for the upcoming week's AQ conversations.

THE SCOOP AND DUMP

PLAY STRATEGY: This play is one of the easiest ways to clean up after your teammates have left. Simply lift the far ends of the tablecloth and bucket all the trash inside. Then throw it all in the garbage or a Dumpster.

COACHING POINT
Pulling off this play requires the AQ to actually have a tablecloth in his possession. If you don't, you may use a blanket instead.

HANG TIME

There is an unspoken amount of time one allots or is allotted to remain at the home of another AQ after the conclusion of the game. You've spent a lot of time together, and, once the final game is over, it's best to vacate. You may use the following formula as a guideline:

Number of Games Watched Together	1	2	3	4
Hang Time (minutes)	30	20	10	5

AUDIBLE

How to Eject Somebody by Using Proper Bouncer Technique

1. Ask him politely to leave the premises.

2. If he refuses, you need to apply physical force. Just make sure you remove any bottles of beer from his hands—you may get cracked over the head or, more commonly, invite spillage.

3. Fold his arm behind his back or apply a headlock. Swiftly lead him out the door.

4. Tell him to have a good night, and close the door.

THE FOOTBALL FUNK

There are few things more psychologically disappointing than a loss. Try to turn your attention elsewhere, such as to a football-related video game—a suitable football distraction and a great deal of fun. It is reasonable for an AQ to feel the loss for a few days, but if the depression or irritability continues much longer than that, the AQ may be showing symptoms of a more serious depressive issue. If you are experiencing problems with family or coworkers more than a week later, you may want to consult a professional. Just make certain to see an AQ psychologist to ensure a fair diagnosis.

AQ FUNDAMENTALS
Football Video Games: Tips from Madden NFL

Wind down and relax at halftimes and after the game with a violent game of video football. (For video football game basics, see the Resource Section.)

Offense:

- Establish the run early; this will help set up the play action, which can lead to one-on-one coverage for your wideout.

- Watch the linebackers as soon as you snap the ball, and check for the blitz. There is nothing worse than looking downfield to throw a pass and being sacked when your tight end or running back is open in the flats.

- When using your QB vision, look off less aware safeties, because they will be more easily influenced by which receiver you lock on to.

- If someone keeps blitzing up the middle against you and you're having a tough time getting the pass off, use the slide-protection pinch to clog up the middle with your offensive linemen.

Defense:

- Have your top cornerback cover your opponent's top receiver.

- Put your top defensive back on a lower-rated receiver. You will limit your opponent's ability to throw to that side of the field. Roll your pass coverage to the other side of the field, and focus on defending your opponent's top receiver.

- If your opponent's passing game is targeting the halfback, you may consider assigning your top linebacker or defensive back to the halfback. That way, you can take or limit the primary threat and force the quarterback to throw to other receivers on the field.

- If you are playing against teams with an elite tight end, you may want to assign a linebacker or a safety with good coverage skills to him.

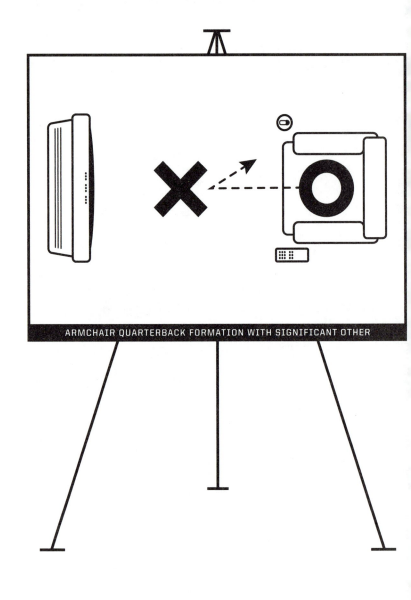

ARMCHAIR QUARTERBACK FORMATION WITH SIGNIFICANT OTHER

CHAPTER 3

SIGNIFICANT-OTHER PLAYS

Some people don't respect the game like you do. There are women—even men—who feel no shame in questioning your game-viewing schedule. Some even have the audacity to plan events during your coveted game time. (Because the majority of AQs are male—though an astonishing number of women are joining the ranks—the significant others referred to in this chapter are female.) Regardless, when a woman chooses to date or marry an admitted AQ, she is also getting hitched to his football team. Therefore, to ensure that there's no misunderstanding, make sure she is aware of your AQing before she makes such a significant life decision. (If you have a team-logo tattooed onto your neck, she should know you're serious.)

MAKE THE CONVERSION

PLAY STRATEGY: Spread the gridiron gospel by teaching your girlfriend or spouse the subtleties and strategies of football. If she doesn't take to it quickly enough, pique her interest with fascinating background information on the game, such as

- a player's charity work
- a fascinating news event related to the game or the team's home city
- the name of a quarterback's famous girlfriend or wife
- an inspirational story from an athlete's childhood

Then, begin to teach her the fundamentals of the game. Inspire—that's what winners do.

BABE BLOCKING

You have a significant other, and you love her. But she must understand that on game days, you want to spend time with your other love. It shouldn't be taken personally, and it shouldn't be a competition. Take the time to show her how much she means to you with an occasional snuggle during *Monday Night Football*. And, to keep things in order, always show her you're attentive with a well-placed *chick check* now and then during game time-outs.

FOOTBALL FLOWERS

PLAY STRATEGY: Every Saturday or Sunday prior to the game, woo your honey with Football Flowers. The Football Flowers power play should relieve much of the haranguing that often accompanies your decision to spend 22 consecutive Saturdays, Sundays, and Mondays watching up to 12 straight hours of football, plus highlights. With the flowers and an occasional card, she may even come to look forward to game day.

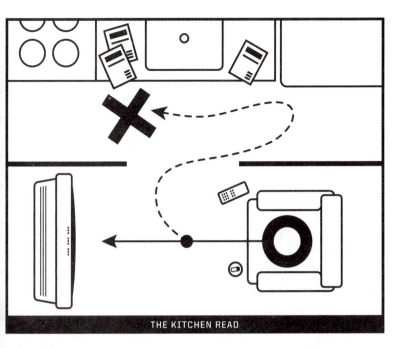

THE KITCHEN READ

THE KITCHEN READ

PLAY STRATEGY: Scatter fresh reading material on kitchen counters—culinary and home-decor magazines, newspapers, art books, and the like—to divert the attention of ladies or non-football fans on game days. Also place materials on the coffee table, just in case an opponent slips into your field of play.

THE LISTEN-AND-RESPOND FAKE

PLAY STRATEGY: Your significant other is talking to you, but there is too much going on in the game to have an ill-timed conversation. Interject generic lines such as these to let her know you're really listening:

· "No, really?!"

· "I totally understand."

· "Then what happened?"

THE FANTASY FASHION LEAGUE

PLAY STRATEGY: Are you being hassled for spending too much time on your fantasy game? Get her hooked on Fantasy Fashion League, an Internet-based game similar to fantasy football in that players draft a fantasy team of designers and celebrities: Giorgio Armani, Donna Karan, George Clooney—whoever. She can join as an individual or with a team of friends. (For more information about Fantasy Fashion Leagues, see the Resource Section.)

> ### AUDIBLE
> ### Six Indications That Your Fantasy Football Commissioner Is Corrupt or Incompetent
>
> · He has new people in his league every year.
> · He seems to always draft before you do.
> · He alters the rules after the draft.
> · He approves of heavily lopsided trades.
> · He is often unreachable.
> · He stalls on payouts.

THE END-AROUND

PLAY STRATEGY: When it comes to placating impatient opponents, always be honest. Buy some time by giving them the facts: "There's only nine minutes left." AQs know that nine minutes includes numerous time-outs remaining, a two-minute warning, replay calls, play stoppages, and commercials, all lasting at least a half-hour or more.

AQ FUNDAMENTALS
Fantasy Football

What do high school students, college coeds, construction workers, Wall Street brokers, and grandpas all have in common? Many are fantasy-football fanatics, and they all should observe fantasy football's unwritten rules:

- As soon as the NFL preseason begins, last year's fantasy-football champion is old news. If you were the winner, your bragging rights have officially concluded.

- However, you may proudly bring your championship trophy to league meetings, because it reminds everyone what's at stake. At home, you may display your trophy in your TV room as a silent reminder of your greatness to yourself or to anybody within its vicinity.

FANTASY GOD

- Discussion of fantasy football is in no way limited to the football season. Fantasy-football players can riff about fantasy football any time of the year. During the off-season, if you are not working on your game 24/7/365, prepare to get crushed by somebody who is.

- Talking about yourself or your team in the third person after a huge win or a championship season is tolerated, but only for two weeks following the game or the season's end.

- If you bring a friend into the league, make sure that he is devoted to playing and that he understands your reputation is on the line. If he bails out early, he screws up the integrity of the game for everyone else. The other players will rail against you, and deservedly so.

THE SAKS SACK

PLAY STRATEGY: Offer your chick a day of shopping with the girls—with the understanding that she won't sink your credit card.

THE GARDEN HOOK

PLAY STRATEGY: Play on your woman's gathering instinct and plant a garden together in the preseason. Then, on game days, give her carte blanche at the nursery to keep her occupied for the day. She plants seeds; you plant yourself in the shotgun formation.

AUDIBLE
Four Questions You Should Never Answer

- "When's this stupid game gonna end?"
- "What else is on?"
- "Who's the teal team?"
- "Why do you care so much?"

TIGHT END DRILL

PLAY STRATEGY: Because you're concerned about your sweetie's health, give her a gym membership at the beginning of the season. The better the physical condition she is in, the better she feels.

COACHING POINTS:
The Tight End Drill is a delicate play, and you must make it perfectly clear to your partner that, though you are buying her a gym membership, you are in no way implying she is fat.

Note: Beware of personal trainers. If some gym rat is touching your girl during the middle of a football Saturday or Sunday, he's obviously not an AQ, so he cannot be trusted.

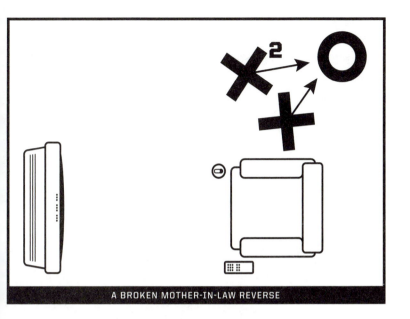

A BROKEN MOTHER-IN-LAW REVERSE

THE MOTHER-IN-LAW REVERSE

PLAY STRATEGY: To show your partner you don't dislike her mother, encourage her to go out to lunch with her mom, and maybe catch a movie together, on a game day. This way, mom and daughter can catch up while you catch the game.

COACHING POINT
Use caution with the Mother-in-Law Reverse, as this is a fragile play. For example, it can backfire into a hazardous situation in which your wife and your mother-in-law decide to get together at your place instead. This can devolve into a frightening game-time atmosphere where they are both attacking you, further drawing you away from the game.

THE *CABARET* CLINCH

PLAY STRATEGY: Surprise your doll with tickets to a popular musical for her and her best friend. She gets *The Sound of Music;* you get the sound of crushing hits.

AUDIBLE
The Master Massage

With the Master Massage, you can soak up the game from your recliner and expertly rub down your girlfriend or wife at the same time. Soon, she may beg for game day. Follow this routine:

1. Sit her down on the floor in front of your recliner so that she is also facing the game, her head fitting between your knees. Have her lean slightly forward, allowing you access to her head, neck, and shoulders. Tell her to relax.

2. Begin with a scalp and facial massage. With your fingers splayed, run your hands through her hair, pulling gently back and forth on her scalp. Slowly work from the base of her skull up to the top of her head. Then move your fingers over her face, massaging her forehead. Draw your fingers down past her cheeks, gently tugging and pulling on her ears. Then work back down the back of her head until you get a firm grip on her shoulders and neck.

3. With a hand on each shoulder, massage the top of both shoulders, working the trapezius muscle with your thumbs and fingers as if adding rub to a steak. Work your thumbs into the middle of her back below the traps, between her shoulder blades.

4. Move your hands slowly toward the tops of her shoulders—her deltoid muscles. Compress your hands on the sides of the delts, gently squeezing each part of the shoulder as you continue downward until reaching the back of her arms. Gently squeeze the arms and then return back up to her traps, head, and neck. Repeat as necessary.

5. During the massage, take a break to gently move her head back and forth in a rocking motion so that the head is bobbling, as if weightless.

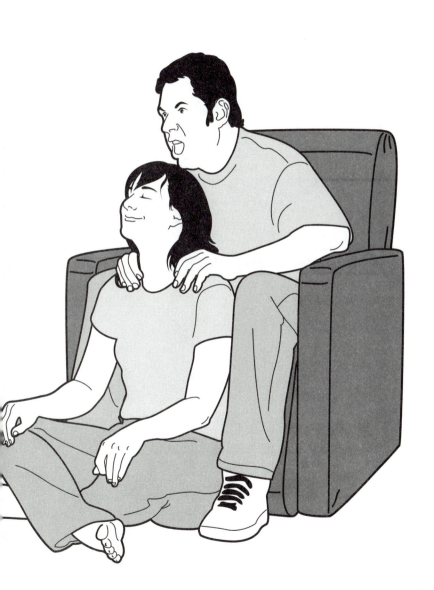

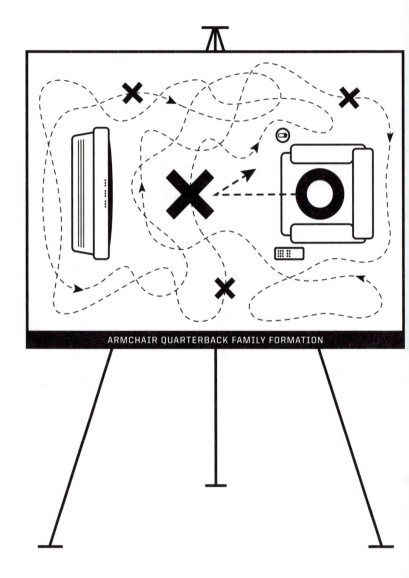

ARMCHAIR QUARTERBACK FAMILY FORMATION

CHAPTER 4

▪▪▪

FAMILY PLAYS

▪▪▪

If you watch games frequently and have a family, chances are your game-viewing schedule has been a source of friction for everybody involved. A household AQ faces many challenges a solo AQ may take for granted. So, for him to succeed, it takes sharp play-calling to overcome parenting obligations.

Having children can severely complicate your AQ game, but parenthood also has its deeply rewarding moments. For example, a proud AQ might have fathered an AQ prodigy—a child who shows tremendous AQ potential and has quickly taken to watching football with his father, perhaps even reciting statistics. (However, the AQ prodigy has his own issues to deal with, such as a bedtime to adhere to, siblings who interfere, or an overbearing mother who believes he's damaging his eyes—a notion that is, in fact, untrue. See page 99.) Another advantage of having AQ children is the initiation ceremony—that emotional day when the offspring is officially welcomed into the sport. Common rites of passage include donning his first official game jersey and devouring his first hot wing.

The rub is that young children require your constant attention, yet so does the game, which means something has to give—and it shouldn't be the game. To put their attention elsewhere, you can execute a simple Draw Play by always having a supply of crayons, paper, and coloring books nearby during the broadcast. Hell, challenge your little tyke to draw a football player!

FAMILY PATTERNS

Or, say your family is putting you on the defense by claiming you never let anybody watch what they want. In these instances you can change the momentum by counterattacking and taking the offense: point out that they get to watch their programs all week long, and all you ask is to watch your games just once or twice a week. If this still isn't enough, you may have to go for the jugular: refer to your pre-prepared list of character defects and past screw-ups, express disappointment, induce shame and guilt, then say that the only thing that can calm you down is watching the game.

But if your family still doesn't get it, you might want to employ the following plays.

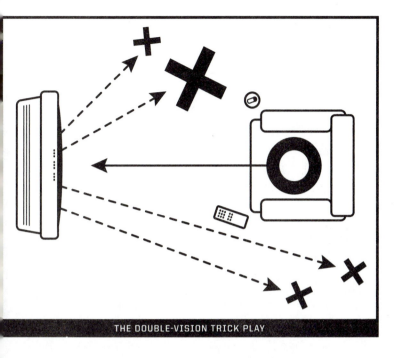

THE DOUBLE-VISION TRICK PLAY

THE DOUBLE-VISION TRICK PLAY

PLAY STRATEGY: Use the reflective surface of the TV to see what's going on around you. With this play, you can maintain direct eye contact with the game, watch your kids, and have sideways vision of a significant other if conversation is required.

THE TOY-TRUCK TUCK

PLAY STRATEGY: Throughout the week, pick up a few toys here and there and find a place to hide them. The moment your son or daughter causes a distraction or, even worse, blocks your view of the game, break out the new fire engine. And, if you're willing to spend a little more, a cool handheld video game can keep your child occupied or addicted for weeks.

INTENTIONAL GROUNDING

PLAY STRATEGY: If your children are whining about wanting to watch their shows on the game TV, use this cunning play carefully, step by step.

1. Develop a look of shock and disbelief on your face.

2. Establish eye contact of no less than 30 seconds with each child involved, in dead silence.

3. Arch eyebrows slowly and ask whether their rooms are clean. (If their rooms are already clean, ask if their homework is complete.)

4. Walk slowly with authority to each child's room. (Pause the DVR if applicable.)

5. Throw open the door, survey the chaos, and tell them there will be no TV privileges until they clean their rooms (or finish their homework).

THE COIN TOSS

PLAY STRATEGY: Bribery is the best policy. When family members are standing between you and your game, you may need to throw some cash at them to remove them from your field of play. Establish a set amount of money to be thrown, and repeat when necessary.

COACHING POINT
Because your spouse or family is spending your money, if you are inclined, you are fully justified in placing a football wager. Think about it: they're spending, but you're *investing*.

THE BABYSITTER PASS

PLAY STRATEGY: As a generous sacrifice, swap an off day with the kids for game days with your teammates. Take the children out; give their mother "her time" in exchange for game time.

AQ FUNDAMENTALS
How to Bet Like a Professional Gambler

Use these sports-wagering fundamentals to maximize your payouts:

- When taking the favorite, bet early in the week. When taking the underdog, bet later. Favorites usually pick up steam from bettors, which moves the point-spread line further against you. The Patriots might be just 8-point favorites on Monday but may jump to 10-point favorites on Saturday. The earlier you get them, the better. Conversely, as more bets come in on the favorite, the underdog will accrue more free points later in the week.

- If you're taking the over in the point total, you should usually bet early in the week. If you're taking the under, bet later. More bets are usually placed on the over, which means a game total that may begin the week at 42 points can end the week at 44. Whether you're taking the over or the under, those 2 points are huge.

- When going against a point spread that has a ½-point in it, try to stay on the good side of "the hook." Football games are often decided by increments of 3 or 7 points, which means when the line is -6½ or -2½ you might be more inclined to go with the favorite, and if the line is +3½ or +7½ you should consider taking the underdog.

- There's more value when you bet *against* popular teams. Certain popular football teams, such as the Dallas Cowboys or Notre Dame, have more wagers placed on them every week. Whether they are the favorite or the underdog, the sheer volume of bets placed on such teams moves the betting line against them, which is not always an accurate reflection of the true handicap.

[For more information about smart sports betting and office-pool software, see the Resource Section.]

Why It's Important for Children to Watch Sports

- Watching the game will teach them how to modulate enthusiasm and depression.

- By rooting for a team, they will learn how to stand up for what they believe in, even in the face of adversity.

- Rooting helps develop strong lung capacity in case your children ever need to scream for help.

- Knowing sports will help develop the all-important skill of backslapping, a prerequisite to entering the boardrooms of corporate America.

THE CLUTTER AND CLEAR OUT

PLAY STRATEGY: Leverage a neat freak's compulsion and free a little game time by cluttering up an area of your home you know your little worker bee will feel compelled to clean. If you are blamed for the untidiness, you may deny it or accuse the children or the dog.

THE "WHERE'S ROVER?"

PLAY STRATEGY: If you are fully engrossed in the game when, suddenly, your children demand to watch an alternate show, you might want to execute a cunning dog-ditch maneuver:

1. During a commercial time-out, take the family dog to your neighbors' house and ask them to keep him for a few hours.

2. Return home and tell the kids Rex is missing.

3. To keep them actively searching for the dog, offer them a cash reward. Then, after the game has concluded, retrieve Rex from your neighbors' house and return him to your house.

4. Depending on your mood, you can hand out the reward anyway or keep the cash for yourself.

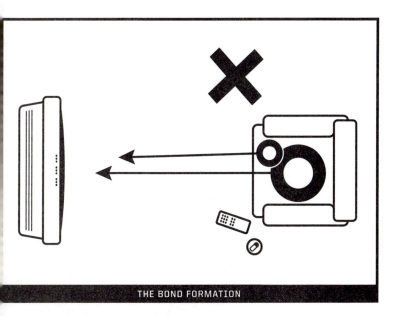

THE BOND FORMATION

THE BOND FORMATION

PLAY STRATEGY: Your wife claims you're not spending enough quality time with your son or daughter. Earnestly explain that you will bond with your child by watching football together.

THE JUNIOR TACKLE

PLAY STRATEGY: Your son is pestering you to play with him. Politely tell him you'll play with him as soon as your game concludes. If he continues, you may want to launch a more aggressive move.

1. Playfully wrestle him to the floor so that you are facing the TV.

2. Keep him firmly pinned, but keep it fun—and, most important, keep watching the game.

COACHING POINT
The Junior Tackle is also an effective play call when dealing with a rebellious teenage son who has chosen the wrong time to challenge your authority.

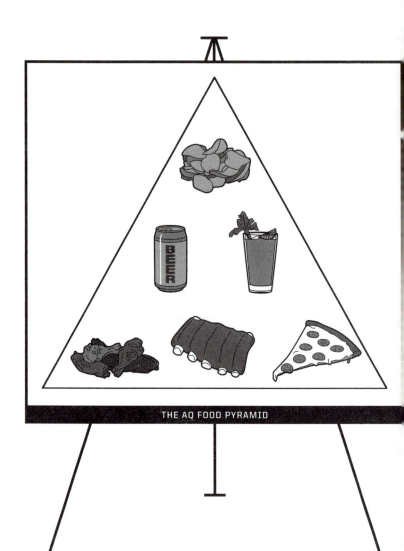

THE AQ FOOD PYRAMID

CHAPTER 5

GAME FOOD

Sufficient energy intake is crucial for the active AQ—even if he appears to be inactive—because maintaining peak levels of inactivity requires substantial energy. An AQ needs his proper nourishment for extreme clicking, yelling, arguing, celebrating, and rising and reclining. Whether you're chilling at home, having buddies over, or going to an away game and you want to bring high-quality offerings with you, here are appropriate AQ foods and beverages for the game occasion.

BEER

AQs and beer go mug-in-hand. Whether you'll be performing for just a few hours or for an entire day, you'll need the proper fluids to help you excel. Experts say to keep your body hydrated on hops, and you'll maximize your game, week in, week out.

Whether the beer is just for you, for the group, or presented as an offering, everyone should adhere to these AQ beer rules:

- *Have enough on hand.* When hosting, you must provide enough beer to last through overtime. If visiting teammates have told you they are bringing beer offerings for the game, you must be sure it will be enough, and, if you're not, purchase some backup brew in case. Having an "understanding" that your buddies will be bringing beer is not worth the risk of not having enough. And, if you live in the Bible Belt or in a state with weekend blue laws, be sure to purchase your alcohol at least a day in advance.

- *Have the right beer.* If you are hosting and you are a nondrinker, consult with a beer drinker as to what brew to purchase for the game. Blueberry wine coolers probably aren't the way to go.

- *Can or bottle?* That all depends on personal preferences and how much you want to spend. However, if there is a chance that violence will break out between teammates through smack talk, consider purchasing cans rather than bottles.

- *Light or dark?* If beer spillage on the carpet is a concern, consider serving light beer instead of dark. (However, a responsible game host would never allow spillage to be a serious issue.)

THE BEER BITCH

PLAY STRATEGY: When the beer is running out, it is essential that a receiver go out deep and deliver for you. To complete this play, assign the teammate who didn't bring beer to the gathering—but is drinking game beer nonetheless—to be the Beer Bitch. If, however, all teammates have brought beer, or more than one did not, the AQ may select the guy who has the best-paying job, as he is the most likely to retrieve a high-quality—and a high quantity of—beer.

TOP DRAFT PICK: THE KEGERATOR

For the beer-advanced, there is the Kegerator—a mini-fridge with an integrated tap that hooks up to a CO_2 tank. You can have crisp draft beer for more than a quarter of the season and it will pay for itself. (For more on Kegerators, see the Resource Section.)

AUDIBLE
Beer Is Healthful!

Great news! Beer is actually good for you. It has no fats and is packed with vitamins. According to many physicians, beer has the following health benefits:

- Drinking a couple beers a night can lower the probability of suffering a stroke or developing vascular problems. Beer contains high amounts of vitamin B_6, which helps the body perform a variety of tasks, including removal of toxic amino acids and maintenance of metabolism.
- Beer bolsters your good cholesterol and reduces the likelihood of blood clots.
- Beer may reduce stress and calm nerves, important for sleeping well after an exhausting day in the armchair.

AUDIBLE
Two Football Drinking Games
The Player Name Game!

During the course of a game you'll hear the same names repeated over and over and over again. So at the beginning of the broadcast, each teammate chooses a player's or coach's name that he knows will be called out often. Every time the announcer mentions the name you have selected, you may force any teammate to drink a swig. Star players, a legendary head coach, or a player who is recently in the news are all intelligent choices.

The Announcer-Cliché Game!

Take a swig every time you hear one of these doozies. If you have the presence of mind to utter a cliché before the announcer does, take extra swigs!

- "no question"
- "smash-mouth football"
- "a great player, but an even better person"
- "coaching genius"
- "poise in the pocket"
- "a class act"
- "well disciplined"
- "second effort"
- "gut check"
- "mental toughness"
- "presence of mind"

HAIL BLOODY MARY

PLAY STRATEGY: Make a large batch of hot effin' Bloody Marys with this blistering recipe.

BAD-ASS BLOODY MARY (MAKES 5 SERVINGS)

INGREDIENTS:

32 oz. can V8 vegetable juice

3 tbsp. white horseradish

2 tbsp. Worcestershire sauce

1 tbsp. Tabasco sauce

1 tsp. celery salt

½ tsp. cayenne pepper

500 ml vodka

DIRECTIONS:

Add all ingredients except vodka and stir heartily.

Add vodka and stir once.

Pour into glasses filled with ice.

Garnish with celery stick.

(For more Bloody Mary recipes, see the Resource Section.)

WINGS

The Buffalo wing originated in 1964, when a Buffalo, New York, tavern owner named Teressa Bellissimo had the idea to deep-fry chicken wings and drizzle them in hot sauce as dinner for her son. Up until then, chicken wings were usually disposed of or used for making stock. Today, wings have quickly become a staple in the AQ diet. They're quick to eat, flavorful, and satisfyingly barbaric—the perfect feast for a barbaric game.

■ ■

TOWEL-ROLL WINGS [MAKES 36-42 WINGS]

PLAY STRATEGY: You don't always have to buy wings—see if you can make them yourself. Cook up this deliciously messy wing recipe for your teammates. And make sure you have a full roll or two of paper towels on the coffee table for considerable hand and face wiping.

INGREDIENTS:

4 tbsp. butter

1 cup Frank's Hot Sauce

2 tsp. Tabasco sauce

1 tsp. cayenne pepper

1 tbsp. tomato paste mixed with 1 cup water

3 lbs. chicken wings, fresh or frozen (if frozen, make sure they are fully thawed)

Ranch or blue cheese dressing

Olive oil as needed

DIRECTIONS FOR SAUCE:

Melt the butter in a small saucepan over medium heat.

Stir in the other ingredients, except chicken wings and dressing, and cook until lightly bubbling.

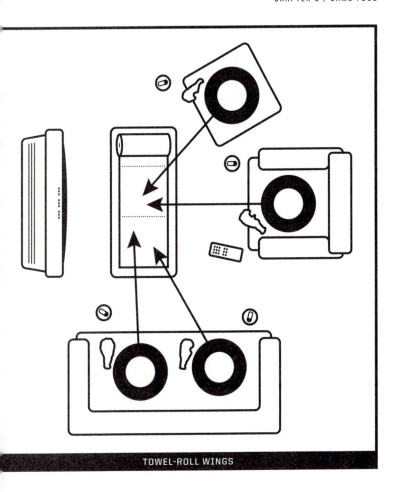

TOWEL-ROLL WINGS

DIRECTIONS FOR WINGS:

Rinse the wings and pat them dry.

Cover them lightly with olive oil and place them evenly on a cookie sheet.

Cook them at 475 degrees Fahrenheit for 35–45 minutes or until they're crispy golden brown.

Remove them from the oven and coat them with the sauce, reserving some of it for the side.

Place them back in the oven for an additional 5–10 minutes.

Serve the reserved sauce and dressing on the side.

AQ FUNDAMENTALS
Wings

- It's better to be safe than hungry. Always order or make more wings than you think you'll need. Leftover wings can be saved for the home AQ or, with the team's consent, taken home by a visiting teammate.

- For easy and more enjoyable eating, try using the "Small Bone and Smash" technique professional eaters employ (see facing page).

- Never use a fork or a knife to eat a hot wing without expecting to be ridiculed. If the wing-eating field of play is set up correctly, there shouldn't even be a fork accessible.

- Never leave an uneaten or half-eaten wing on your plate, no matter how hot it is. This is not only wasteful; it's disrespectful to the wing bringer, your hungry teammates, and, on a deeper scale, the chicken.

- Buffalo wings come in two forms: the drumstick and the wing. You should not hoard one or the other unless your teammates have been informed of your preference and agree to it.

- Wings can be consumed solo or as a part of a balanced meal with blue cheese or any other dipping sauce (with the exception of hummus), regular fries or curly fries, and celery, and can be washed down with beer or soda.

- No matter how many wings you consume, they're still only considered an appetizer—allowing for additional pizza and meat consumption.

RUSSIAN WINGETTE

PLAY STRATEGY: If you and your chums have the stomach for it, play this balls-out game of guts wherein super-hot, nuclear wings are mixed in with your table's normal temperature of wings. One-by-one, pick your wing, eat it, and hope the wing gods are good to you. [See How to Swallow a Burning Hot Pepper, page 83.]

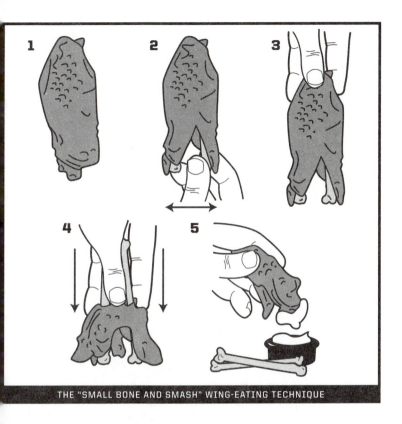

THE "SMALL BONE AND SMASH" WING-EATING TECHNIQUE

THE "SMALL BONE AND SMASH" WING-EATING TECHNIQUE

PLAY STRATEGY: Maximize your wing meat intake and make life easier with this smart eating technique employed by the pros.

1. Use the wing portion, not the drumstick.

2. Twist the small bones apart on one side.

3. Stand the wing like a tripod.

4. Push down hard revealing just bones and the good piece of chicken meat.

5. Dip as necessary.

AUDIBLE
How to Eat 100 Buffalo Wings

At least one month prior to game day:

- Eat plenty of leafy foods such as lettuce, cabbage, or collard greens daily.
- Exercise to speed up your metabolism.
- Begin stretching your stomach. Eat one huge meal a day, such as a buffet, over the course of a few hours, and always wash it down with plenty of fluids.

On game day:

- Be relaxed, and eat at a consistent pace—20 wings per quarter and at halftime. Drink a quart of water per quarter and at halftime.
- Use the "Small Bone and Smash" technique (see page 81) to make the wing eating more manageable.
- Burp often to get the air out.
- Soak up the glory and adulation of your teammates.

(For information about Philadelphia's annual Wing Bowl, see the Resource Section.)

WINGA

PLAY STRATEGY: Play Jenga with your wing bones in this *wing*ineering contest among teammates. With a steady hand, stack your gnawed-off bones on top of each other on a wing bone plate. The AQ who places the wing that causes the growing pile to come crashing down must purchase the subsequent order for the table.

AUDIBLE
Wing Slang

Wing enthusiasts have a language all their own. Here are a few examples courtesy of Cluckbucket.com:

- *Drummie:* The leg portion of the chicken wing.
- *Wing:* The two-boned portion of the wing. Also known as "the flat" in the Northeast and Southeast areas of the United States.
- *Nub:* The often discarded portion of the chicken wing found directly opposite the drummie.
- *Nibble Meat:* The little pieces of meat and breading left over by an AQ's date or child who is too finicky to finish—good for swabbing excess sauce.
- *Naked:* Chicken wings without breading.
- *Wet:* Hot wings with a large amount of sauce on them.

AUDIBLE
How to Swallow a Burning-Hot Pepper

You've ordered the nuclear chicken wings, and, after eating one, strangely, your mouth is on fire. Why? Because they're cooked with lethal habanero peppers, literally 100 times hotter than Tabasco. You've just swallowed capsaicin, the basis of the hot pepper plant's natural defense system. It rapidly heightens your taste sensation and pain sensitivity, and then blasts your mouth with a burning-hot agent. Thankfully, you can cool the intense burning—not by drinking water, but by eating or drinking dairy. Immediately consume one or more of the following:

- A lot of ranch or blue cheese dressing.
- A glass of milk.
- A cup of yogurt.
- A scoop of ice cream.

GRIDIRON GREATNESS

AQ superstars want to be in the action every minute of the game. Yet with the grill on the outside and the game on the inside, is it possible? Certainly. Rule the BBQ throughout game day, feed yourself and all of your teammates, and don't miss a second of the games with this highly-advanced back-to-back-to-back gridiron trifecta.

■■►

HALFTIME HAMBURGERS [MAKES 6-8 SERVINGS]

PLAY STRATEGY: If you're a person who loves football, research indicates there's a strong likelihood you love hamburgers too. After two quarters of wing gorging, you're about ready for some dessert. Begin your streak of gridiron greatness with the following Halftime Hamburgers.

INGREDIENTS:

2 lbs. ground chuck or ground round

½ cup ketchup

2 tsp. Worcestershire sauce

2 tbsp. grated onion

3 tbsp. bread crumbs

BEFORE THE GAME:

Combine the ingredients in a bowl.

Shape the mixture into 6-8 large burger patties.

DURING THE GAME:

At the start of the 2-minute warning, place the patties on the grill and cook them at medium heat for 5 minutes per side, or until done, as desired. The burgers will be ready by halftime.

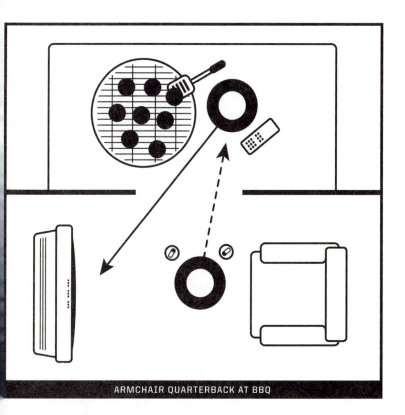

ARMCHAIR QUARTERBACK AT BBQ

THE SECOND-GAME STEAK

PLAY STRATEGY: You've watched the early game and worked up an appetite worthy of an AQ. Now, you have a 10-minute window between games. Use your time wisely and fuel up for game two with a good steak.

If you didn't cover the spread last week and money's tight, you can filet your friends by substituting a high-quality piece of flank steak and passing it off as filet mignon. Flank steak is more affordable, yet is still a hearty piece of meat. And nobody needs to know.

For an added touch, you can prepare a gallon of Second-Game-Steak Marinade the day before.

CONTINUED ▶

THE FLANK FLICKER [MAKES 5 SERVINGS]

(If you prefer to marinade for extra flavor, follow the Second-Game-Steak Marinade recipe below.)

INGREDIENTS:

2 lbs. flank steak

¾ tsp. kosher salt

½ tsp. ground black pepper

DIRECTIONS:

Season the flank steak on both sides with salt and pepper.

Grill the steak on medium-high for 6–10 minutes per side, depending on desired doneness.

Remove the steak from the grill and let it sit 10 minutes before slicing.

SECOND-GAME-STEAK MARINADE [MAKES 1 GALLON]

INGREDIENTS:

3 cups sugar

2 qt. pineapple juice

2 qt. soy sauce

12 oz. red wine vinegar

2 tbsp. minced garlic

BEFORE THE GAME:

Combine the marinade ingredients.

Place the thawed steaks in large plastic bags.

Add 2 cups of marinade.

Marinate the steaks in a refrigerator for anywhere from 3 hours to 3 days.

DURING THE GAME:

Put the steaks on a medium grill during the 2-minute warning of the second half of game one. The steaks will be ready when game one ends. (Cook them at the preferred temperature for 5–12 minutes.)

AQ FUNDAMENTALS
BBQ

Lavishing your teammates with delicious BBQ is a classy gesture, but with manning the grill on game day comes great responsibilities. Here are the laws of the gridiron:

- Nobody is to touch the griller's meat. As with his remote control, the home AQ alone is to operate the grill, unless he has delegated BBQ duties to a teammate. (Note: when an AQ goes outside to man the grill, he may also designate his remote control to his most trusted teammate, or, if he has a powerful remote, he can remain in control from the grill.)

- If the AQ is barbecuing for his teammates—a wholly generous gesture—his teammates are required to immediately update him on critical game situations and scoring changes as they happen.

- The griller's teammates will serve him beer as soon as his bottle is empty. He shouldn't have to ask.

- If the griller is not cooking the food properly, he may be stripped of his tongs, but only after a consensus has been reached among teammates.

GAME-THREE RIBS [MAKES 5 SERVINGS]

PLAY STRATEGY: The early games are over and the second slate of contests is NFL history. The evening match-up is still to come—but not for 90 highlight-filled minutes. Digest the last football game of the day with a delicious 5-pound rack of baby back ribs—have them ready just in time for the game-three kickoff.

INGREDIENTS:

5 lbs. baby-back pork ribs

2 tbsp. brown sugar

2 tsp. chili powder

2 tbsp. vinegar

2 tbsp. soy sauce

CONTINUED ▶

BEFORE THE GAME:

Mix the ingredients (except the ribs) in a small bowl.

Rub the mixture on the ribs with thick coats on both sides.

Put the ribs into a refrigerator.

Warm up the grill as soon as game two concludes.

Put a rack of ribs on the warmed-up grill 15 minutes later.

Grill the ribs bone side down over low to medium heat and cook for 1½ hours, basting often.

The ribs are done when you can stick a fork between two of them and separate them.

Serve the ribs just before the game-three kickoff (after they've been cooking on the grill for 60–90 minutes).

LINEBACKER'S CHILI [MAKES 6-8 SERVINGS]

PLAY STRATEGY: A finely tuned team of AQs needs hearty proteins to perform their game-day plan successfully. Whip up this batch of AQ sustenance prior to game time for the energy you'll need to guide your men to victory.

INGREDIENTS:

1 tbsp. vegetable oil

½ cup chopped onion

½ cup chopped green bell pepper

1½ lbs. lean ground beef

1 envelope (1¾ ounces) chili seasoning mix

½ cup water

1 can (14.5 oz.) diced tomatoes, undrained

1 can (15 oz.) kidney beans, undrained

1 tbsp. tomato paste

DIRECTIONS:

Heat the oil in a large, heavy skillet.

Add the chopped onion and green bell pepper and sauté them lightly.

Add the ground beef and cook it over medium heat until it is no longer pink.

Drain the oil.

Stir in the chili seasoning mix and add the remaining ingredients.

Bring the chili to a boil.

Reduce heat, cover, and simmer for 10 minutes.

Serve with chips.

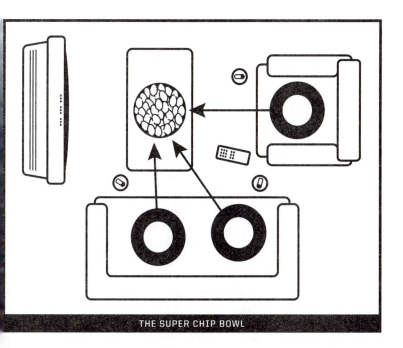

THE SUPER CHIP BOWL

THE SUPER CHIP BOWL

PLAY STRATEGY: When you have teammates over, it is acceptable to pour chips into a large bowl and place them somewhere in the center of the room. The benefits follow:

· Friends don't have to bark for chips.

· Having them in a bowl eliminates distracting bag noise.

· Having them in a bowl reduces crumbs on the floor.

COACHING POINT

Many AQs would consider pouring a bag of chips into a bowl an unmanly play and a gross mismanagement of time, but it truly makes sense. Excessive chip bag noise can muffle critical sounds of the game, such as a jarring hit or an important ref's call. Plus, you don't need dirty man hands diving into the bag and soiling or destroying the chippage. If you are harassed as a wuss, deny the player the chips until he repents.

STRONG MAN SALSA [MAKES 2½ CUPS]

PLAY STRATEGY: Who needs bland, store-bought salsa when you can pull off a fresh play like this one?

INGREDIENTS:
- 2 cans (29 oz.) diced tomatoes
- 1 can diced green chiles
- ¼ cup fresh parsley or cilantro
- ¼ cup thinly sliced green onions
- 2 tbsp. lemon or lime juice
- ⅛ tsp. pepper
- 1 clove garlic, minced
- ¼ tsp. salt

BEFORE THE GAME:
Drain the tomatoes, reserving only ¼ cup of the juice.
Combine the tomatoes and the juice with the remaining ingredients
Cover and chill the salsa for at least 4 hours.
Serve the salsa with tortilla chips.

AUDIBLE
The Training Diet

If the standard AQ diet is not suiting your waistline, there are easy ways to shed excess poundage—generally preferred by female AQs or by males who like to eat like females. Note that utilizing these techniques may open you up to criticism. (See the proper bouncing procedure on page 52.) Slimmer substitutions may include:

- pretzels instead of chips
- dips with low-fat yogurt, not sour cream
- raw nuts rather than chips
- apples, grapes, or cherries* in lieu of candy
- light beer

*Be careful not to choke on the pit of the cherry when reacting to a play or a call.

THE VAZQUEZ PLATE

PLAY STRATEGY: Use your armchair ingenuity to create a Vazquez Plate, a makeshift plate that holds both your beer and your food. Named after its inventor, Marc Vazquez, this highly functional dishware allows you to stay mobile with your grub (chips, wings, and so on) using just one hand, freeing up your other hand for high-fives, remote-controlling, and finger flippage. Follow these directions:

1. Start with a thick, sturdy paper plate. Fold in half.

2. Cut—or bite—out a hole in the center of the plate that is the circumference of your beer container.

3. Place the beer through the hole. It should fit snugly inside so that it won't fall through.

4. Fill the plate around the beer with chips, wings, or any other food choice.

5. Walk freely with your food and beer together.

6. Sit back down, place your Vazquez Plate on a nearby table or your lap, pull your beer from the center hole, and consume.

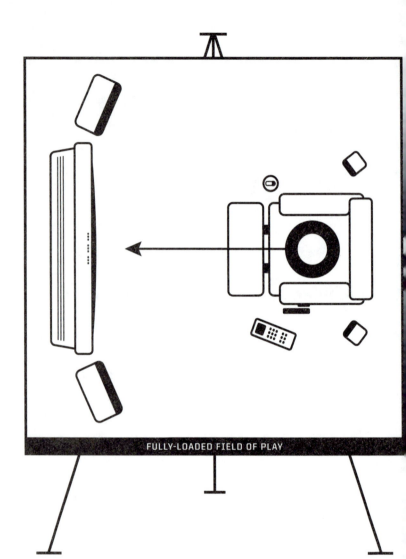

FULLY-LOADED FIELD OF PLAY

CHAPTER 6

THE EQUIPMENT ROOM

The modern AQ has been blessed with an arsenal of high-powered weapons to play with; it all depends on how much you want to spend on your franchise. But as long as you have a chair and a TV, your primal needs are being met. The rest is just very cool football dressing. (For more information about AQ home-theater equipment, see the Resource Section.)

THE RECLINER

The snug, cushy back comforts you, fitting your contours like a tailored suit. As you lean back, its footrest raises your legs and elevates your football soul. And on game day, you work together as a unit—synergistic, fluid, efficient.

The recliner was invented in Monroe, Michigan, by a pair of cousins in 1928. According to AQ lore, the two had just been to the "talkies" and had viewed a football-game reel featuring Notre Dame's legendary Four Horsemen. Crammed into uncomfortable theater seating, the cousins quickly ascertained that they would be much more at ease viewing football while leaning back in a cushioned chair with their feet propped up, so they went home and began designing their vision. These men understood the posturing of the AQ, and, in 1937, the cousins received a patent for the world's first automatic armchair recliner, and founded a company—La-Z-Boy.

■■

THE SHOTGUN

PLAY STRATEGY: You *can* have it all. Set up your *I formation* with a decked out Italian-leather number that includes a 10-motor massage, lumbar support, a heating system, a wireless WAN, a Dolby stereo, caller ID, and a built-in thermoelectric beverage cooler. (For more information about deluxe recliners, see the Resource Section.)

THE GRAVITY BACK

PLAY STRATEGY: Ergonomic recliners are available that allow you to take the weight off your legs so that you are in a weightless position even as you put on game weight. This seating reduces the stress on your heart improves blood circulation, soothes muscle tension, and relieves pressure on your spine. It takes a talented AQ to operate the clicker or zip a football around with his teammates from this zero-gravity position. (For more information about zero-gravity chairs, see the Resource Section.)

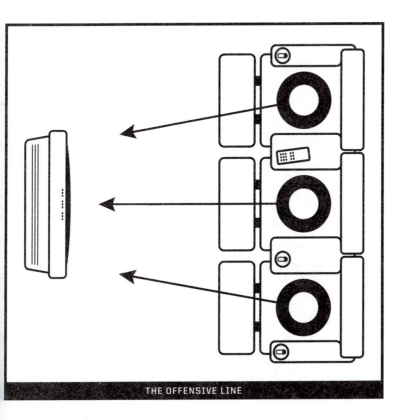

THE OFFENSIVE LINE

THE OFFENSIVE LINE

PLAY STRATEGY: Imagine sitting with your teammates side-by-side-by-side in fully-equipped multiseat recliners. Move in unison, react as one, be a unit, look beside you and know that your teammates have your reclining back all day long. With an intimidating front four such as this, you'll always be confident that nobody can get between your boys and your game.

AUDIBLE
Shopping for Seating

When shopping for a recliner, pricing, room size, decor, and fabric, and the recliner's size are all factors to consider. Your body and your recliner should perform in a fluid synergy, an economy of motion allowing for optimum AQing performance. Here are some tips to help you purchase the perfect armchair:

- *Consider the fabric.* Leather is smooth and sleek and won't get blotched by beer or salsa spills, but it's also more expensive. You can spend less by covering your recliner with a suede look-alike such as microfiber, or you can protect your investment with a simple Scotchgard treatment. Then again, an armchair's stains are like game-day scars that add character.

- *How equipped?* Decide what extra AQ features you want and need, such as a built-in fridge, an integrated phone, a back massager, and any other luxury you should have. When an AQ masters his recliner's features, it's a sight to behold.

- *Hop in and give it a test drive.* Before you purchase a chair, try out every feature and mechanism to make sure they will deliver in the clutch. The last thing you need is an injured recliner you'll have to replace mid-season.

- *How much room do you have?* What good is a recliner if it's backed against a wall? Map out your floor plan and the space available before you go to the store. Let the salesperson take it from there.

- *The right fit.* The armchair should complement the AQ's physical measurements—height, weight, and frame—for optimum comfort and playmaking ability. If your legs can't reach the floor, you're going to have a difficult time using your recliner.

PLASMA OR LCD?

Many AQs consider a plasma-screen TV the medium for the premier game-viewing experience. In fact, it is widely believed the plasma screen's inventor was a Japanese AQ.

Plasma upsides:

- Larger screen sizes and wider viewing angles offer more depth of the football field and more viewability for your friends all around the room.

- It has a better contrast ratio and renders deeper black.

- Team colors appear richer.

- There's more seamless play tracking when you DVD.

Plasma downsides:

- It's expensive.

- Videogaming or excessive broadcast graphics may leave burned-in images.

- It doesn't operate as well at higher altitudes.

- It has a shorter shelf life.

LIQUID-CRYSTAL DISPLAY (LCD)

Introduced in the early 1990s, this breakthrough technology immediately mesmerized AQs nationwide. As men were shopping in electronic stores, they became so entranced by the lifelike LCD screen showing a football game that many found themselves unable to leave the store for hours, until the game had concluded.

LCD upsides:

· Lower prices.

· There are no burn-in static images.

· It has a cooler running temperature.

· It works better at higher altitudes.

· Its display is brighter.

· It has a longer display life (twice as long as a plasma TV).

LCD downsides:

· None.

(For more information about TVs that are ideal for watching football, see the Resource Section.)

AUDIBLE
Vision Quest

Contrary to what you may have heard, if you watch correctly, viewing hour after hour of football games on TV isn't at all harmful to your eyes. But you can't be careless, as any serious AQ understands that his eyes are his most valuable assets. Follow these tips, and you can watch games for your entire life:

· Position your TV at eye level.

· If you've been staring at the TV for a lengthy period, take a moment to look away (a great time to acknowledge your children and your better half).

· Keep your TV room properly lit. Too much light reduces the contrast on the screen, and too little may fatigue your eyes. Avoid colored lights and lights that glare off the TV.

· Don't strain at the running box-score scrolls after 11:30 P.M

· Do your eyes water when you watch a game? Unless you've lost a substantial amount of money, there might be a larger problem, so consult an optician. The good news is that there are special viewing glasses designed just for watching TV that help eliminate tearing and prolong an AQ's career. If your teammates mock you for crying during the game, tell them they are tears of rage and that you'll kick their asses if they mention it again.

CABLE OR SATELLITE?

As a modern AQ, you're not asking for much—all you demand is the right to have thousands and thousands of hours of football coverage for next to nothing. For factors ranging from pricing to programming, cable and satellite have their own advantages and disadvantages. Use these tips to help you decide.

· *Pricing.* If you have three or more TV sets in your home, you might consider cable, because it's most cost effective. With satellite, you need an extra receiver for every set, for which you must pay additional costs every month. If you require only one receiver, satellite is probably the better value.

· *High-speed Internet options.* Sometimes cable providers offer a discount on high-speed cable Internet access. Consider going with cable if it's important that you monitor your fantasy-football stats.

· *Signal interruptions.* Adverse weather can impact satellite reception and result in static or a distorted picture. Usually, the interruptions are brief, but if one occurs during a big play, it can be disastrous. Losing your game because of a downpour or an ice storm is no joke. If your cable goes out, it can sometimes take hours to get the line repaired, putting the lives of cable guys at risk.

· *Ask around.* Quality of service can vary widely in different areas, so seek out your neighboring AQs to learn of their experience with cable and satellite.

· *Football-package options.* Look at the options for your area—your favorite team may be televised only via cable or satellite.

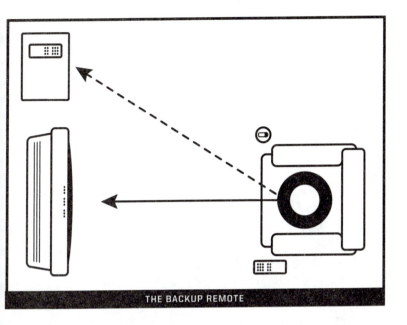

THE BACKUP REMOTE

THE REMOTE

The remote control is one of the AQ's most indispensable pieces of equipment—even if your remote isn't in your hand, your fingers know instinctively where it is. From his reclined position, armed with his clicker, the AQ can deftly operate his entire arsenal of audio and visual equipment instantaneously. Following are some tips for maintaining maximum control of your game.

■■

THE BACKUP REMOTE

PLAY STRATEGY: Always carry an extra remote on your roster. Losing your clicker before or during the football broadcast can be a frightening feeling, and an AQ might experience a desperate sense of loss of control. Where the hell is it?! It could be buried deep in the sofa. Perhaps a daughter, feeling ignored, swiped it out of spite and is holding it hostage.

Once you get your spare, hide it carefully. Stash it in your toolbox or humidor or somewhere your family won't look. (For more information about duplicate remote controls, see the Resource Section.)

THE UNIVERSAL FEED

PLAY STRATEGY: Streamline all your remotes into one ultrapowerful clicking machine. If you don't have a backup remote or are unable to purchase one because yours is outdated, get the universal remote and it will replicate the signal required to run your TV and other equipment. Do a Web search of the model number of your remote control (or your TV), and there's a good chance it's out there. (For more information about universal remotes, see the Resource Section.)

THE REMOTE GUARD

PLAY STRATEGY: Consider creating a plastic cover for your remote made from a clear plastic bag or cellophane to keep it from getting gummed up. Also, qualified remote technicians can fix problems such as keys that don't work, gummy keypads, fried circuit boards, and defective parts.

AUDIBLE
The Emergency Radio

Equip yourself with an emergency radio in case of a power or cable outage, or if you are going to an event and you need to hear your game. AM bandwidth is a necessity and will allow you to pick up all local games. A shortwave bandwidth will help you listen to more distant games around the country and even overseas—ideal for the NFL Europe aficionado.

AQ FUNDAMENTALS
The Remote Control

- *No clickerjacking.* One may never use another AQ's remote control without his consent. When a visiting teammate brazenly uses another AQ's clicker without his permission, punishment might include slugs to the shoulder or, depending on the channel he's landed on, temporary removal from the field of play.

- *Responsibility.* A great deal of accountability comes with being the remote controller during the game, but no responsibility is more critical than channel selection. If the home AQ is not landing on the correct games, is late to return to them, or, perhaps most alarming, is not even watching football, visiting teammates can force the offending AQ to give up his remote.

- *Game juggling.* When the main game of interest is approaching blowout proportions, it is appropriate to change to a lesser important, yet more competitive contest on a different channel. Also, when the main game goes to commercial the remote controller is expected to quickly switch to a different live game until the primary game returns from commercial break.

- *No throwing the remote at the TV.* You're angry. Your quarterback just tossed a devastating interception or blew coverage on a critical third down. But heaving your remote at the TV can only break your clicker and damage your TV. If you must, whip your remote at soft objects such as a couch cushion or even a fan of the opposing team.

AQ FUNDAMENTALS
DVR

Digital video recording is a revolutionary advancement with tremendous football-watching benefits. You can be your own instant-replay man, pause and rewind live game action, review great plays and scoring drives, re-listen to an announcer's call, and record multiple games. However, with such awesome power comes the need for restraint:

- *Don't get lazy.* Watching the broadcast as it unfolds live should always be the first priority of an AQ, and, as such, his DVR should be used only as an accessory to the game-watching experience.

- *Catch up quickly.* Your friends might call to discuss a current play, which can mess with your game equilibrium, so get up to real time ASAP.

- *Obtain pause approval.* If you're watching the game with teammates and seek to pause the live action, you must garner majority approval. Others shouldn't suffer just because you have to use the restroom. (See the Open-Door Slant, page 39.)

- *Establish DVR recording priorities.* Make sure your girlfriend/spouse/roommate does not have her or his shows ranked higher to record than football. Nothing's worse than tuning in to the game only to find the latest TV medical drama in its place.

A GLOSSARY OF ARMCHAIR QUARTERBACK VERNACULAR

■■■

AQ SNEAK

Sneaking a peek at the gyrating cheerleaders without letting a significant other notice.

BACK CRACK

The fleshy exposed rear end of an AQ, often brought on by *crack back*.

BARELY AUDIBLE

An extremely low volume level allotted to an oppressed AQ who lives under the TV rules of another. The *barely audible* also applies to a volume level for those with young, sleeping children. (See *Oppressed AQ*.)

BEER BLITZ

The all-out rush to the cooler, refrigerator, or grocery bag that houses the game-day beer. [See Illegal Return, page 35.]

BLADDER LATERAL

Urination sprayed in any direction other than the bowl line. More cases are reported during the fourth quarter than during any other segment of a game. [See Open-Door Slant, page 39.]

THE ARMCHAIR QUARTERBACK PLAYBOOK

BLIND SIDE
The part of the TV that is unviewable due to sun glare.

BOOT BONK
The shanked punt executed by an AQ outside during halftime.

BOTTLE BURNER
The rash one gets from trying to open a twist-off beer-bottle cap between his forearm and his biceps.

CHEAP SHOT
One who brings food and beer only for himself, or one who eats as much as anyone else but commonly neglects to pitch in for food delivery. [See Visiting Plays, page 28.]

CHEER BLOCK
When the presence of a significant other impairs an AQ's ability to share in the *good cheer*.

CHICK CHECK
During a stoppage of play, talking to, calling, or texting a girlfriend or spouse to let her know you're thinking about her.

CLICKER FINGER
Malady caused by repetitive finger stress brought on by extreme remote-controlling. [See Finger Flex, page 21.]

CRACK BACK
A vertebrae-snapping mid-game torso twist to relieve the back tension of an AQ who lacks mobility.

EXTRA POINTS
Scoring good favor from significant others by executing a smart offensive game plan. [See Football Flowers, page 56.]

FLANKER POSITION
The position of the teammate on the far right or far left of the formation, who has the worst view of the game. [See The Ottoman Swipe, page 37]

FLOODING THE FIELD

When the men at a holiday gathering pounce to watch the football game as soon as the TV is turned on. [See Thanksgiving Football Traditions, page 48.]

GAS OUT

Claimed or unclaimed flatulence in the field of play.

GOOD CHEER

The welcome sight of gyrating cheerleaders smiling at the AQ. [See Acceptable Talking Points During Blowouts, page 40.]

HASH MARK

A cigar-ash stain left on the field of play.

HINTERFERENCE

When a significant other uses unwarranted sexual innuendo or physical contact in an attempt to interfere with an AQ's ability to follow the game.

I FORMATION

A seating formation in which an AQ is perfectly centered in front of the TV, either solo or with his teammates at his sides in a symmetrical formation. [See The Shotgun, page 94.]

OPPRESSED AQ

One who struggles to live under the oppressive TV rules of a non-AQ. He may be an AQ mooching a couch from a pal or an adult still living with his parents, perhaps burdened by financial issues while having to contend with a disappointed father. (See *Barely Audible*.)

PERFORMANCE ENHANCERS

Substances that can intensify the game, such as alcohol or tobacco.

REMOVING THE CHAINS

Using smart game plays to free oneself from a significant other or the family to watch the game.

REVERSING FIELD POSITION

When an AQ switches the focus and majority of game time from one game to another. [See Game Juggling, page 103.]

SHE-Q

A female AQ. [See Make the Conversion, page 56.]

SHOVEL PASS

Getting the OK to watch the game from a significant other after shoveling snow all morning.

SPORTSCENTERRHEA

The affliction of watching football highlights over and over on an overnight loop and remaining interested.

STIFF-ARMING

When an AQ uses strength and intimidation against an opponent to secure a seat, the remote control, beer, or food.

UNBUTTON HOOK

The unzipping or unsnapping of the pants while watching Thanksgiving football. [See Thanksgiving Football Traditions, page 48.]

VOLUME BLOCKING

To shut out the incessant chatter of a roommate, nagging of a significant other, or noisy children by simply raising the volume of the game to an extremely high—even blaring—level.

WAIVER SLICE

To swipe the last slice of pizza by claiming nobody else wanted it.

WARNING SHOTS

Pounding alcohol during the 2-minute warning to prepare oneself for a very tense finish.

RESOURCE SECTION

BEER: ALLABOUTBEER.COM

Beer is the AQ's Gatorade. Information about lagers, ales, stouts, pales, brewing, beer fests, beer talk, and more can be found on this comprehensive Web site for the beer guy, courtesy of *All About Beer* magazine.

BLOODY MARY RECIPES: DRINKSMIX.NET

The ultimate Web site for everything Bloody Mary—the perfect football-Sunday morning and afternoon refreshment. This site offers more than 20 classic and contemporary Bloody Mary recipes, from Bloody Mary punch to the Bloody Biker.

BROADCASTING: *SPORTS BROADCASTING*, BY BRADLEY SCHULZ

You call the play-by-play before the announcer does. You drop football anecdotes better than Dierdorf. Who says you can't be a football announcer? Check this book out. Covering all aspects of sports broadcasting, this text discusses reporting, writing leads, style, tricks of the trade, shooting on location, editing, producing, live event production, ethics, and résumé tapes, as well as tips on seeking employment in the industry.

CIGARS: CIGARAFICIONADO.COM

A smooth game cigar is a smooth play. Get a knowledge drop at *Cigar Aficionado* magazine's Web site. It provides basic information on the manufacture, care, and appreciation of premium hand-rolled cigars.

DOG TRICKS: FISHLIKEFISH.COM/DOG-TRAINING

If you've never had the pleasure of your dog serving you a beer, learn this amazing trick right here. You'll learn that it doesn't take a smart dog—just a patient AQ. If your dog already knows how to fetch and drop objects, he's already halfway home with your brew.

FANTASY FASHION FOOTBALL: FANTASYFASHIONLEAGUE.COM

It's cute. It's pink. It's cutthroat.

GRILLS: BBQ.ABOUT.COM

Be a gridiron great. The helpful article "Barbecues & Grilling" breaks down the best gas grills for game day by quality and price so you can find the perfect grill for Saturday and Sunday feasts.

HOME-THEATER SETUP: HOMETHEATERMAG.COM

Deck out your field of play with all the home-theater goodies you found out about at *Home Theater* magazine's Web site. This decadent site helps you build your setup from the ground up and features buyer's guides, equipment reviews, shopping tips, news, blogs, and links.

KEGERATORS: KEGERATORS.NET

You can never have too much beer. That's why you can build a Kegerator using an old refrigerator. Follow the instructions on this Web site to install a standard refrigerator to make the perfect home draft beer system. Or you can simply purchase one, though it is recommended that, so as to avoid shipping damage or faulty equipment, you buy your Kegerator at a retail store rather than online.

OFFICE FOOTBALL POOLS: WAGERTRACKER.COM

If you work in an office, you probably enjoy office football pools—not only for the weekly competition, but also because football pools invite football talk, which is much more engaging than actual work. If somebody else is putting the pool together, that's great for you, but if you're the guy, use this free office-pool software. It can be set up in minutes, allowing you to run your own office pool with minimal effort.

ONLINE SPORTS BETTING: BETCRIS.COM

You don't have to go to Vegas—or even leave your recliner— to find great football betting lines with immediate payouts. This is one of the world's leading international sports books, fully licensed and regulated. Ultracompetitive prices and fast, friendly, and efficient service make it tops in the industry. However, online gambling is always subject to U.S. regulations.

PAINTING TEAM COLORS: MOSTCOLORFULFAN.COM (THE HOME DEPOT)

For a grandiose home-field facility, paint your TV room's walls with your team's logo. The Home Depot offers a sports-themed paint line called Team Colors that boasts more than 400 paint colors representing 76 NFL and NCAA teams. The Web site, owned by the Home Depot, features a virtual room for you to try out your color combinations, as well as painting tips, plus a store finder to get you started. Perfect for college dorms and for homeowners who want to raise their home's retail value.

PLASMA DISPLAY VS. LCD: AUDIOHOLICS.COM

The modern AQ lives in the gilded age of televised football. But it's getting hard to keep up with edgy TV technology. Learn the differences between LCD, plasma, DLP, LCOS, D-ILA, and CRT TVs and displays in this online magazine's Display Technologies Guides.

RECLINERS: ASKMEN.COM

Buying a new recliner is like bringing a new teammate home. Fits, fabrics, styles, pros, cons, and most everything else are reviewed in the article "Your Guide to Buying a Recliner" on the online magazine AskMen.com.

REMOTE CONTROLS: REPLACEMENTREMOTES.COM

Losing control of your game is not an option. If you want to score a replacement, a backup, or an omnipotent universal remote, this Web site should have what you need: it stocks nearly every brand. If you still don't see your clicker, though, there's a quick and simple remote-finder option.

SPORTS BETTING: *SHARP SPORTS BETTING,* BY STANFORD WONG; SHARPSPORTSBETTING.COM

Done in moderation, there's nothing wrong with betting on sports. It's legal, it's fun, and, yes, you can win. Want a complete lesson in betting on the NFL? For the beginner, this book explains how to place bets, money management, calculating what you stand to win on bets, and what types of bets are available, including separate chapters on money lines, over/under bets, props, parlays, and teasers. Check out Wong's Web site, too.

SPORTS BARS: *SPORTS ILLUSTRATED*, FEBRUARY 4, 2005

You never know when you're going to need a good sports bar. In this issue, *Sports Illustrated* does exhaustive research and offers tips on finding the perfect sports bar in its article "The 25 Best Sports Bars in America." (The top choice: Boston's The Fours.) A book titled *The Guide to America's Best Sports Bars* is available on Amazon.com, but its content is somewhat dated.

TVS: DLPTVREVIEW.COM

Your TV means a lot to you. Should you purchase at a brick-and-mortar store, or online? Do you go to a major electronics chain, or a specialty boutique? Check out the article "Where Should You Go to Buy Your DLP TV."

VIDEO GAME FOOTBALL: VGSTRATEGIES.ABOUT.COM

Before you can destroy your friend in video football, you have to learn the basics. Use the tips, strategies, and other information in the article "Football Games 101: A Guide to Football Video Games Basics" to take your videogaming to new heights.

WING BOWL, PHILADELPHIA, PENNSYLVANIA:
610 WIP RADIO, (215) 592-0610

Founded in 1993, the Wing Bowl is an annual event that pits competitive eaters in buffalo-wing gorging of epic proportions. It's traditionally held on the Friday preceding the Super Bowl at Philadelphia's Wachovia Center and draws over 20,000 rabid fans. If you think you're ready to compete, you can gain entry by performing a stunt on a Philly radio show, where you must consume a prodigious amount of food—say, 20 Big Macs. Or you can be granted automatic entry into the Wing Bowl with a victory at a sanctioned 2-minute "wing-off" between other hopefuls. Thong-clad Wingettes serve the wings and serve as eye candy. The record is held by Joey Chestnut, who ate 173 wings in 27 minutes at Wing Bowl XIV.

WINGS: CLUCKBUCKET.COM

Ready to wing it? This is considered to be the best chicken wing Web site in the world. It includes chicken-wing eating techniques (featuring devouring tips from renowned professional eaters), a chicken-wing dictionary, merchandise, and blogs.

WOMEN AND FOOTBALL: GET YOUR OWN DAMN BEER, I'M WATCHING THE GAME! A WOMAN'S GUIDE TO LOVING PRO FOOTBALL, BY HOLLY ROBINSON PEETE

If football is starting to get in the way of your relationship, maybe it's time to turn your girlfriend or wife into a football fan. Holly Robinson Peete, wife of ex-NFL quarterback Rodney Peete, teaches the game and its origins and answers all the questions women have about football in fun, easy-to-read, engaging prose. Soon enough, your lady might want to sit down and enjoy the game with you.

ZERO-GRAVITY CHAIRS: HOMEDICS.COM

Watching football can be stressful. Zero-gravity seat positioning helps reduce back and muscle strain, improves circulation, and can dissolve tension in your shoulders, back, thighs, and legs. Visit this Web site and find a store locator near you. As with any recliner, just make sure you test-drive it first.

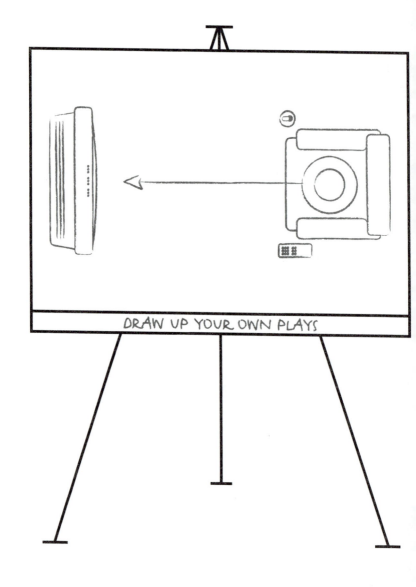

DRAW UP YOUR OWN PLAYS

THE CHALKBOARD

Are you an Armchair Quarterback playmaker? An offensive guru and a defensive wizard? An innovator and a leader? Use these pages to draw up the plays and schemes that take your game to the next level. Or just use the pages to scratch notes. E-mail your plays (drawn up or written out) to ArmchairQuarterbackPlaybook.com and share your "coaching genius" with the Armchair Quarterback nation. Your plays could even be written into the next edition of *The Armchair Quarterback Playbook!*

PLAY STRATEGY:

COACHING POINT

PLAY STRATEGY:

COACHING POINT

PLAY STRATEGY: _____

_____
_____
_____
_____
_____
_____
_____
_____

COACHING POINT

_____
_____
_____
_____
_____

PLAY STRATEGY: _____

_____

_____

_____

_____

_____

_____

_____

_____

COACHING POINT

_____

_____

_____

_____

_____

PLAY STRATEGY: _____

_____

_____

_____

_____

_____

_____

_____

COACHING POINT

_____

_____

_____

_____

_____

PLAY STRATEGY:

COACHING POINT

PLAY STRATEGY: _____
_____
_____
_____
_____
_____
_____
_____
_____

COACHING POINT
_____
_____
_____
_____
_____
_____

PLAY STRATEGY: _____

_____
_____
_____
_____
_____
_____
_____
_____

COACHING POINT

_____
_____
_____
_____
_____

PLAY STRATEGY: _____

_____

_____

_____

_____

_____

_____

_____

COACHING POINT

_____

_____

_____

_____

_____

PLAY STRATEGY:

COACHING POINT

PLAY STRATEGY:

COACHING POINT

PLAY STRATEGY:

COACHING POINT

ACKNOWLEDGMENTS

■■■

Thank you to all of my friends and family for their continual support; Chronicle Books and sensational editor Matt Robinson, whose vision and sense of humor helped guide this project from day one; and the renowned Mike Essl, for bringing my words to life with his outstanding design and illustration. Thank you to all of the Armchair Quarterbacks and experts who shared their knowledge and passion with me throughout the process of crafting this playbook, including writer-extraordinaire Ben "Benvy" Applebaum; Dave "Value-Added" Bilyeu; Laurie "The Yogi" Cooney; "Seven-Letter" Heather Braunstein, who helped inspire the title as well as the author; John "Silver & Black" Buturla; the wily AQ veteran Bobby Buzcek; Robert "Pinnin'" Feldheim; Ken "Kenspiracy" Flood; Kenny "Kivorka" Friedman; master marketer Glenn Gang; Stephanie "The Restaurant" Garbutt; the Madmen at Man Laws; Mark "Livin' la Vida" Livolsi; Jaime Luna fish; headshot hotshot Myles Maher; promotion savant Mike Mancini; the visionary Marc Alexander Vazquez; Laura, Michael, Jonah, Sarah, Oscar, and Nelson Weintraub; the invaluable Victoria White; and Mark "Soft Hands" Williams.

8034325